THE RUNT

by
RICK BOYER

D0871103

Contents

Chapter 1

KIT HUNT, RUNT

My name is Kit Carson Hunt and my father is the sheriff of Barry County. Kit isn't my real first name; Carson is. But when I was just a nubbin, everybody started calling me Kit Carson and it just stuck. Ever since I've been old enough to know about Kit Carson, I've been proud of the name, so I never minded.

Daddy named me after his deputy, Bud Carson. That's because Bud saved his life one time. It was before I was born, but I've heard it told about a lot of times. Everybody, almost, likes my father, so when Bud saved his life it made Bud a hero all over Barry County. As the story goes, Daddy had been called out to break up a fight between two men out in front of the courthouse. Cassville is the county seat and so whenever people have a quarrel they can't settle, that's where they go to swear out warrants and such on each other. Most disagreements could be resolved without bothering Judge Blaylock. They'd go at it with fists, and if that didn't settle it, they'd go at it with rocks. If that didn't settle it, they'd go at it with knives. Usually, it didn't go as far as the courthouse.

1

But this one day, there was a misunderstanding between Bernie Sloan and Jake Flatt that got clear out of hand. Bernie had butchered a hog that Jake claimed as his own. Lots of people had hogs running loose in the woods in those days, and sometimes it got mixed up as to what hog was whose. That's the way it was now, with Jake claiming that the black-and-white hog Bernie had butchered wore Jake's ear notch. Bernie said no, the hog had an ear that had been torn in a fight or on barbed wire or something, and wore no ear notch at all. He claimed the hog had been born in his own hog lot, and he had just never got around to ringing or marking it.

Old Jake had said that Bernie was so stupid that whipping him wouldn't even be a fair fight, though he himself was thirty years the older of the two. So he was going to take Bernie to court to make him pay for the hog. Unfortunately, the day he went into town to file papers, he ran smack into Bernie and the matter was unexpectedly settled out of court.

It was mighty strange that the two of them should meet like that; neither one of them normally being in town more than once or twice in a given month, and neither one of them expected to run into the other. But sometimes those things happen, and you just can't ever tell.

They say Jake was just about to cross the street to the courthouse when Bernie walked out the door of the general store and ran smack into him.

"Hey, why don't you watch where you're a-going!" Bernie sputtered, staggering back a step. Then the two men recognized each other.

"Well, I might of knowed it," growled Jake. "I reckon any feller that don't know other people's hogs from his own

2

wouldn't have sense enough to walk down the street without runnin' over somebody."

Bernie's meaty face turned red. "Are you callin' me a hog thief, you possum-faced old buzzard?" he roared.

"No, I ain't a-callin' you a hog thief. I'm a-callin' you a hog thief and a loafer and a no-good ignorant jackass, that's what I'm a-callin' you!" Old Jake stood there, lean and weathered-looking in his black coat, nose to nose with Bernie and not backing up an inch. "And if that don't suit ye, I'm goin' across the street to the courthouse right now to break you from suckin' eggs. I'm a-gonna git me a warrant and a sentence and a writ of Hideous Corpus and I'm a-gonna git your flea-bit carcass throwed in the pokey!" He rasped all this out in his high-pitched, nasal voice, gesturing with both hands and ending in a shout like a temperance preacher.

That was more than Bernie could take. He was generally known as a moonshiner and a brawler and a chicken thief, and like other upstanding citizens he wasn't about to have his good name stomped in the dirt. He set his poke of dry goods down on the sawmill plank boardwalk and commenced to roll up his sleeves while Jake whipped off his coat and threw it over a nearby hitch rack. Then both men stepped into the dirt of the street and began slugging.

Jake got in the first lick, which was a considerable advantage, but Bernie was a big fellow and shook it off and tied right into him.

A crowd gathered quickly, as anybody would know it was going to. There never was much excitement in a little one-horse town like Cassville. And the show was worth watching. Jake and Bernie were really churning dirt, fists thudding, kicking at each other's shins, filling the air with grunts and growls and language they normally reserved for special occasions.

Finally, somebody got tired enough of watching that they were willing to leave the show and go call the sheriff. When my father arrived from his office a block down Main Street, the two men were still going strong, all wrapped up in each other and rolling around in the dust of the street so that clouds of it rose into the air. Daddy shouldered his way through the spectators and grabbed Jake's foot to try to pull him away from Bernie, hollering at the men but not being heard. Finally he got Jake's attention at least, and the old man rolled to his feet and began berating Daddy for interrupting the thrashing he was sure Bernie needed. Bernie was back on his feet, too, in just a flash and yanked a knife out of his boot. He jumped toward my father, who was shoving Jake toward the opposite side of the street and so had his back turned to Bernie. It was one of those things that happens in a split second—enough time for everybody to see what was happening, but not enough time for anybody to do anything about it.

Evidently, Bernie was mad enough at Jake so that he had some mad to spare for my father, too, for getting in the way of the fight. To this day, everybody who was there says that Bernie would have gotten that big knife into Daddy's back if it hadn't been for Bud Carson.

Bud had been in the office, too, when word came about the fight. But he was a little slower about getting out of the office because he had been in the process of locking up the gun cabinet at that moment, and stayed long enough to finish, then ran out with the key ring still in his hand. It was a big key ring, the old fashioned kind with about thirty heavy keys on it. Only four of them ever got used, Daddy said, but since nobody could remember what the others were for, they didn't dare throw any of them away. It was lucky for Daddy that they hadn't.

When Bud came shoving through the crowd around the fight, Bernie had just pulled his knife and jumped to his feet. Bud saw right away that he would never have time to get between Bernie and Daddy's back, and he couldn't pull his gun and shoot with folks standing all around. So—almost without thinking, he said later—he did the only thing he could do. He threw the keys.

Bernie was in mid-jump when the keys took him upside the head. Arnold Wilson, the barber, was there that day and told his customers for years afterward how those keys hit Bernie's head with a *ching!* that sounded just like a cash register.

Bernie yelped like a kicked dog and threw one hand to his bleeding forehead, but didn't drop the knife. In a second Bud was through the line of spectators and pitched into Bernie like a bobcat. I've always said Bud could outfight any man in the country except my father, and back then he was younger and maybe even more spry than he is now. Anyhow, he looked up to Daddy and they were the best of friends. It took four men to pull him off Bernie, and when they did, Bernie didn't want any more. The knife had disappeared. Old Jake and my father had set their differences aside by then, they were so shocked by the ferocity of Bud's attack. They stopped shoving each other and turned to stare. The four men holding Bud had their hands full, and Bernie still wanted more distance between him and the deputy. He didn't take time to get to his feet, but crawfished backwards in the dirt, making very impressive time for a man traveling on his hands, heels and the seat of his pants.

Later, when they told my father how Bud had come out of nowhere and saved his life, he swore up and down that if Mama produced a boy when she came to term that September, he was going to name his new son after Bud. And that's why I'm Carson Hunt. But everybody calls me Kit.

As I said before, I'm proud of my nickname because of how I got it. Oh, somebody probably called me Kit when I was too little to even remember it; I don't know. But I'm sure the name would never have stuck if Daddy hadn't started calling me by it. The reason he started calling me Kit was, he said, because I was just like old Kit Carson the scout. From the time I could walk on my own I wanted to be in the woods. I was fascinated with everything outdoors. I always wanted to be in the woods hunting or tracking animals, or down on Flat Creek fishing or trapping. Indian lore was my main interest, and I spent most of my indoors time reading about Indians and wilderness skills. And I learned a lot, some from books Daddy bought or borrowed for me, and a lot of it from older men. Daddy was a good woodsman, and so was Bud, who spent a lot of time at our house. Even when I was just a little kid, Bud had the patience to hunt arrowheads down by the creek with me, and answer so many boyish questions that he must have had a hard time not telling me to shut up and let him think once in a while. Between him and my father, I would have learned to be a skillful hunter and fisherman without a lot of effort. But I wanted more than that.

I wanted to be the best woodsman in the county. I wasn't going to be satisfied with your plain everyday accomplishments—catching an unusually big bass now and then, and the like. I was going to be just as much a scout as my namesake, the real Kit Carson. So I studied my Indian books, wore out Daddy and Bud, and worried the old men of the neighborhood nearly to death with questions.

By the time I was ten, I could track as well as any grown man I knew. I could catch fish when everybody said it was too hot for them to bite, and catch good sized ones, too. I knew how to twist a rabbit out of a hole with a forked stick, catch a possum with a snare, or rig a deadfall trap. I buried a groundhog skin in wood ashes to burn the hair off, then cut it into strips for shoestrings. I could shoot the eye out of a squirrel, and nearly always did. I liked hunting, but I couldn't stand to make an animal suffer, so I always waited to fire until I was sure I had a dead shot.

It's funny how things sometimes seem to move sort of in a circle. Looking back, I think another reason I worked so hard at being like Kit Carson—aside from the fascination I had with the woods and such—was that I was like the old scout in a way I didn't like nearly as well. I was little.

Daddy explained to me one time that the reason Kit Carson got the name Kit was that he was small, like me. "Kit" comes from the beaver trade that Carson was in, a kit being what they called a baby beaver. I sometimes suspected that Daddy had size in mind as much as anything when he nicknamed me Kit, but I never asked him. If it was true, I didn't want to know.

It's not any fun being the littlest boy around. You can't do some of the things the other kids can do, or can't do them as well. I couldn't hold my own in wrestling matches because all my friends were bigger than I was. They could all run faster too, what with their longer legs. At least, they could outrun me for a couple hundred yards. I always thought I could keep up with the best of them if we'd go a mile or two, but nobody ever wanted to try long distances. They said they were running for fun, and that wasn't fun.

You get laughed at when you're little. And even when they don't mean anything by it, grown people sometimes make you feel bad by talking about your size. Like the time I climbed up on Widow Jones' roof and put out a fire that chimney sparks had started among the wood shakes. When I came down, feeling all proud and important, she gave me a big hug that crackled my spine, then said something that took the wind right out of my sails.

"Land sakes," she sings out, "saved by a ten-year-old!"

I'd been twelve at the time.

You also get picked on when you're little, especially by people like Eddie Sloan. Bernie Sloan's son, Eddie had carried on the family tradition of brawling and usually found some boy smaller than himself to brawl with. Eddie was the oldest boy around who still went to school. He was about fifteen. He was almost as big as his father and strong, too, with his father's beefy looks and a permanent scowl on his face.

He had whipped me twice, once in town and once when we ran into each other at the swimming hole. I was no competition for him at all, being much lighter and half a head shorter. But that was the kind of fight Eddie was looking for; one he knew he could win. I had surprised him the second time, sticking with the fight longer than he expected me to and leaving him some things to remember me by. It hadn't been that I was so brave or tough; I just knew from the first time that there was no mercy in him and that I had to give him my best shot or he'd jump on me every time he saw me. I kept my distance when I could.

I told Stanley Gillespie, the wagonmaker's son, about it one time when we were in town. I had noticed that Eddie never bothered Stanley, and wondered why.

"Oh, Eddie used to be hard on me. Just like he is on everybody. We used to live close to the Sloans, and Eddie whipped me just about every time he caught me out." He sat beside me on the edge of the watering trough in front of the hardware store and kicked at a dry horse apple with his bare toe. "I finally broke him of it."

I stared at him. "You broke him? How?"

"Honed my knife up sharp enough to shave with and started carrying it open in my pocket. One day he grabbed me and started pounding on me. So I got an arm around his waist, pulled out my knife, reached around and sliced him right across the tail. He let go of me in a hurry and he ain't said boo to me since."

It sounded like a good idea to me, but I knew what Mama would say. Love your enemies, turn the other cheek. I had never even told my parents about Eddie's bullying, because I felt guilty not finding a cure for it myself. But there was no doubt how Mama would feel about cutting somebody with a knife. She always said there was never any excuse to fight unless your life was in danger or you were protecting somebody else. Otherwise, you should walk away from a fight. She didn't say what to do about somebody like Eddie, who would walk right after you.

So I reckon part of the reason I tried to be better at being like Kit Carson than anybody else was because I was

9

trying to make up for being little. I didn't like being small, in fact I reckon I just didn't like myself. Mama tried to make me feel better, telling me that God knew just how to make people on the outside so they'd grow right on the inside. I knew she meant well, because Mama always meant well. And I figured there was probably something in what she said, though I didn't really understand it and just acted like I did so she wouldn't feel bad. But in spite of all her reasons, I never could get over the feeling that I'd been cheated and that God must not like me as much as the other boys because He hadn't made me able to run as fast or jump as high or wrestle well or so many of the other important things there are to do in life. I thought about it a lot and it bothered me a lot.

Once when I asked Daddy if I'd ever get as big as the other boys, he told me that he himself had been a runt. That surprised me, because he's an inch over six feet now, and nearly two hundred pounds of lean meat. His swarthy complexion and shiny black hair speak of his Indian blood, although there's nothing Indian about the curl in the hair. He said that he had been fifteen years old before he had reached a hundred pounds in weight or five feet in height, and that I should just be patient and see what the good Lord did with me before He was finished. That made me feel some better, but I was afraid to count on it. Just because he'd finally grown big, that didn't mean I would. So I kept right on worrying and struggling with it, and trying to find ways to show that I was just as tough and manly as the other boys.

Mama seemed to feel my hurts even when I didn't say anything about them, and I know she felt bad that I felt bad. One day, when I'd come home scowling after having been laughed at by some town boys, Mama took me aside and talked to me. She told me that she had been praying that the Lord would bring something into my life to show me that I was made just right, and didn't need to worry about my size. I couldn't make any sense out of her reasoning, but it was one of those times when her hands felt good as they tousled my hair and pulled my face into her apron. At that moment, something in me felt like her prayers would someday be answered. Maybe her faith trickled into me through her hands; I don't know, but I wouldn't doubt it.

Mama's mother, old Granny James always says that the Lord works in mysterious ways. I reckon she knows what she's talking about, because when the answer to Mama's prayers came, it was in the form of a mixed-breed hound dog pup. It happened the year I turned thirteen. The pup didn't quite seem to fit in, just like I didn't. And just like me, he was a runt.

Chapter 2

BIG NEWS

Simmer Downs was my very best friend. He lived a mile and a half down Flat Creek from us, the other side of Star City. Simmer and I were friends because we lived closer together than almost any two of the other boys except the town boys, and because Simmer was just so easy to get along with. I'd thought about it a lot because he was one of the few kids I knew who never made me feel bad about being a runt. I'd decided that it was possible not to necessarily like Simmer, but nobody could really dislike him very much. Simmer was the most easy-going person I ever knew, just about. He never did anything you could get mad at, except when you were mad or upset about something and he wouldn't get mad or upset along with you. Seemed like he just couldn't be bothered to get excited about anything.

That's why he was called Simmer. His real name was George, but he was so laid-back that his daddy, who was a teaser, was always telling him to simmer down and be quiet. Mr. Downs usually said something like that when Simmer looked like he was already about to fall asleep

12

sitting up, anyway. Simmer was stocky, with a thick neck and a round head that seemed even rounder because he always kept his hair cut short and bristly. He was bigger than me, though we were only six months apart in age. But he never seemed to notice. That suited me just fine.

One Saturday when we were twelve, Simmer and I were walking up the dirt road from the creek to my house. We were feeling pretty good about ourselves, loaded as we were with a dozen fat bluegills and a big goggle-eye on a willow switch stringer. We'd left our poles and lines up in the limbs of a sycamore tree beside the creek where we always did, so we didn't have to carry them back and forth to the house. It was one of those summer days when the world just seems all right around you, like a shirt that fits with nothing binding or rubbing you. We were talking dogs.

"I don't know, Simmer. Target's mighty good just like he is." Target was Simmer's brindle feist dog that we hunted squirrels with.

"Maybe so. I just wonder about the idea of crossin' him with some kind of hound to get a pup with a better nose. Here, I'll take a turn with them fish."

I didn't argue. The fish were getting heavy. Simer took one hand out of his pocket and took the string from me. He let the fish flop against his leg as he walked, smearing the leg of his overallls with slime and scales. He wouldn't smell so good later as his mama saw it, but he didn't seem to notice.

"What did your grandad say?"

"He said he wouldn't. Said a part-hound dog wouldn't get around in the brush as fast. Said it'd give the squirrel more room to run, so's he could take his pick of trees and find one with a knothole so you couldn't shoot him out of it."

"I reckon there's sense in that."

"Yeah. Grandad knows a lot more about it than I do." Simmer spat through the gap between his front teeth, raising a tiny cloud of red dust on the dry surface of the road. It looked like we could use a shower of rain. "How're you doing on getting a dog of your own?"

"Don't know. Our black and tan gyp's in season, so Daddy's asking around about a good dog to breed with. I keep trying to talk him into letting me have one of the pups for my own, but he says with Susan and the two young dogs, he's got all the dogs he wants to feed."

"So what's he want pups at all for? Goin' to sell 'em?"

"Yep. He thinks with Susan being so good, and the young'uns coming along so good too, it'll be easy to sell any more pups she has. And I 'spect he's right. I wish he'd let me have one, though."

This was one of my long-time daydreams, to have a coonhound of my own. I'd never had my own varmint dog, and I could just see myself and my dog bringing in pelts by the wagonload. With coon skins selling for four bits apiece and possums nearly as much, I'd soon have money for that repeating rifle I hungered for. With a good dog and a good rifle, I'd be king of the woods. And Simmer and I would be one step closer to our goal of moving out west to fight Indians. We only lacked our guns, horses and some spending money.

If only Daddy would let me have one of the pups! Our gyp dog, Bruisin' Susan, had built herself a reputation that spread all over the county. On a silvery winter night her bugle voice could be heard for miles, ringing through the rocky hollows of our Missouri hill country, baying to the accompaniment of her big feet shuffling through the hock-deep, frost-brittled hardwood leaves. Daddy and I would be close behind, carrying my single-shot rifle and a lantern to be lit when the coon treed. If the tree could be climbed, it was my job to scramble up and shake the coon out so the dogs could get at it.

My father had added the Bruisin' to the front of Susan's name because she could kill a coon quicker than you could say Jack Robinson. That's not easy to do, because a coon can fight like a Comanche and is covered with a loose fur coat that acts like a soft form of armor. A dog can do a lot of biting on that thick, loose coat without ever getting a good hold on the coon. Meanwhile, the coon puts his needle-sharp teeth to good use and many a dog carried the marks of a coon fight for life. But Susan was the best of the best when it came to fighting, and she had a top notch nose, too.

But I wanted a dog of my own. I wanted to hunt coons of my own so I could sell hides of my own and have money of my own. Trapping paid some, but I wanted more. It was hard to find a job of work that paid in our neighborhood, even when I could get away from the farm chores. But I could hunt at night. Besides, a boy wants his own dog. Boys are just that way. And I would train my dog to be the best tree dog in the country, even better than Bruisin' Susan. I was the best eye tracker around, and my dog would be the best nose tracker. I would name him Chief.

"Who's that?" Simmer startled me out of my daydream, stopping in the road to shade his eyes with his free hand and look ahead toward a man on horseback coming toward

15

us from the direction of town. I stopped too, squinting my eyes against the late morning sun. We didn't get a lot of visitors living three miles from town, and if the rider was headed for our house it could be a matter of interest. We stood watching as the man approached. He was jogging along at a quick trot, about as far from the house in the other direction as we were, maybe a quarter of a mile or so. He slowly drew closer, coming around the curve of the road that ran along the base of the hills bordering the creek bottom. When I could see the white sock on the horse's near hind foot, I knew who it was.

"Why, it's Bud," I said to Simmer. "Now what's he doing out here when he's s'posed to be in town covering for Daddy on Saturday?"

I could feel myself getting excited. Bud must be coming out to talk to my father about sheriff business. And it was something that couldn't wait until Daddy was in town again on Monday. Simmer was thinking the same thing, and we both started walking again, faster than before. Bud trotted his horse on past the house and came on toward Simmer and me. That was like him, Bud liking boys as he did.

"Howdy, men." Bud called out, reining his horse down to a slow trot, then a walk and finally a stop. The horse stood blowing. I liked the way Bud addressed us as "men."

"Howdy, Bud," I said.

We stopped again, looking up admiringly at the deputy. All the boys liked Bud. He was friendly, and he talked to us as equals even though we were kids and he was a middle-aged man, I believe about thirty years old. The horse he rode was a high-stepping gelding he had picked up in Texas when he and my daddy were in the Texas Rangers after the War. The horse was a tall sixteen hands, a true brown, no red in it, with a blonde mane and tail and the one white sock. The saddle was a fine one, not a Texas or Mexican saddle, but some other Western type that looked light and comfortable to both horse and rider. It was covered with fancy tooling and shiny doo-dads that made it look like it was worth almost as much as the horse was.

Bud sat easy in the saddle like a born horseman. He rested his hands on the saddle horn and leaned forward as he talked to us. His catch rope was near his hand and the gleaming butt of his Winchester seven-shot rifle protruded from the saddle scabbard. The butt of a well-oiled Navy Colt .44 could be seen above a worn leather holster on his right hip. He wasn't a fancy dresser like some of the young town dandies, but his clothes fitted him perfectly. With his Stetson hat, broad shoulders and high-heeled boots, he looked to me like an illustration of a Texas Ranger in a dime novel. Someday I'd look like Bud.

"Your pa home, Kit?" he asked me.

"Yessir, far as I know. We've been down at the crick last few hours, so I'm not sure. But it's getting about dinner time, so he should be coming to the house if he's been out in the field someplace."

Bud grinned, his teeth flashing in the tanned face. "I try to time my visits for dinnertime. Us bachelors'd starve if we didn't get some woman's cooking once in a while."

I didn't wait to see if he would tell his business. "What d'you need with Daddy today?" I asked him.

"Got a telegram for him." He patted his shirt pocket. "From the state prison at Springfield. Says some feller escaped from up there and they think he was headed this way trying to get across the line into Arkansas and then

17

west into Indian Territory. They want some help tracking him down."

"No foolin'!" I looked quickly at Simmer and he looked back at me, both of us beginning to get wide-eyed and happy. This sounded promising.

"'At's right. Prison man's on the way down on the train. They say he's bringing a bloodhound with him."

"A bloodhound!" Simmer said, his eyes wide open now. I knew what he was thinking. I was thinking the same thing—that we had never seen a real bloodhound before, and that if one of them was coming to Barry County, there must be big excitement in the making.

"Yep." Bud shifted to a more comfortable position in the saddle and hooked his right leg over the saddle horn. "Looks like we might have a real manhunt around here."

We talked for a few minutes about what it might be like to organize a county-wide manhunt and work with a a bloodhound. All we knew about the sad-eyed hounds was what we had picked up reading Ned Buntline novels and such wild stories, and we didn't know how much to believe. I felt myself getting all shivery and lightheaded thinking about it. It was a good feeling, standing in the May sunshine in the middle of the red, rocky Flat Creek Road that wound its way through the hilly countryside. Talking to good friends, holding a string of fish and feeling the warm spring breeze. But the best thing of all was the prospect of adventure that had popped into our lives so suddenly with seeing Bud ride his horse around the curve of the road.

"Well, I better get on up to the house and find the boss." Bud threw his leg back over the horse's neck and gathered up the reins. "I'll see you fellers in a few minutes."

We watched him turn his horse and lift him into a short lope heading back to the house. The two almost seemed to be floating on air, if it hadn't been for the sound of the hoofbeats.

"Did you see that?" Simmer asked me. "He just touched a rein to that horse's neck and he spun around and took off on one foot! Did you ever see a horse broke so good?"

"No, but when I get my own coon dog you and me're gonna hunt pelts and sell 'em until we've both got a horse like that and a good repeating rifle, too."

"And get us jobs as deputy sheriffs!"

"After we get back from the West, fighting Indians!"

"Comanches!"

"Apaches!"

"Scratchies!"

"Or any other kind! Come on, let's go see about this manhunt."

Bud didn't beat us to the house by much, because we turned up the steam to get there before he could tell Daddy all the interesting details of the escape story. We needn't have worried though, because we beat Daddy back to the house by ten minutes. He had ridden out into the back pasture to see if our little Jersey milk cow had dropped her calf yet. He had finally found her in the woods at the edge of the field with a newborn calf beside her. It had come just in the last few hours, so recently that the calf wasn't on its feet yet. The hooves of a calf are just about the last body parts to develop inside the mama cow, so if the calf is born a little too early, often its hooves will be too sensitive to hold its weight and it will take several hours before it can stand.

19

Daddy had decided to leave them out since the weather was pretty and there didn't seem to be any problems with the calf, but he had been so enchanted with the sight of the baby Jersey with its shiny little black nose and big innocent eyes that he had sat his horse and just taken in the sight as if he were mesmerized. That was like Daddy. And it allowed Simmer and me to get in on the conversation about the bloodhound man from Springfield.

We were sitting on the front porch when Daddy rode around the house and tied his horse to the hitching post by the front picket fence, Bud in Mama's porch rocker and Simmer and me in the swing.

"Well, Bud, what brings you out here?" Daddy said as he swung his long leg across the horse's rump and dismounted.

"Business, boss. Got a telegram for you from the prison at Springfield. Seems they need help catching an escapee."

Daddy took the telegram Bud handed him and sat down on the porch, his boots resting on the top step. He read for a moment then looked up at Bud.

"Says here Sergeant Lew Jenkins from the Bureau of Prisons will be in this evening on the train with a tracking dog. We're requested to find him a place to stay and help him organize the manhunt. There's some other stuff too," his voice trailed off as he lost himself in the telegram again. He absently shoved his hat back from his forehead and chewed the drooping end of his black moustache. Finally, he refolded the paper and placed it in his shirt pocket. "Well, boys, looks like we've got a job ahead of us. You can go to town with me later if you want and we'll bring Jenkins and his fancy mutt out here to the house to stay until we get the hunt going. Right now, my nose tells me dinner's ready, so..." But before we could all get up Mama was at the screen door asking what was the matter that we weren't hungry. We didn't waste any more time.

Half an hour later, Bud pushed his chair back and reached up to get his Stetson off the hat rack. "Well, boss, I'll get on back and hold the fort. Want me at the depot to meet Jenkins with you?"

"Wouldn't hurt, Bud. I've got to stop and serve a summons on my way in, and if I have any trouble finding the feller it may make me late. If Jenkins comes and I ain't there, take him to the office and tell him I'll be along directly."

A moment later Bud had disappeared around the curve of the road at a mile-eating trot. Daddy went on about his afternoon chores and Simmer and I climbed up into the hayloft to talk about the big excitement that was just about to start. We never remembered we had left our string of fish in the front yard until one of the barn cats came up to join us with a bluegill's head in her mouth. She crouched in the hay and started crunching happily.

Chapter 3

BLOODHOUND BUCK

It seemed that the afternoon would never get by, but finally Daddy sent Simmer and me to hitch up Henry and Henrietta, the big-footed plow horses, to the wagon. We forked some hay in the back because there was only enough room on the seat for two or three people, and we wanted to ride comfortably. The ride to town was a lark, except that we had to stop at Bernie Sloan's house to serve a summons on him. Sloan's house was a ragged log-and-board shack with cracked window panes and a sagging front porch roof. The yard was scratched bare by chickens and dogs. One rake-ribbed hound raised his head to look at us from his resting place on the porch but didn't bother to bark. He seemed as shiftless as his owner.

"I wish Daddy hadn't stopped here," I groaned. "You'd think he'd be in a hurry to meet this prison man and get the manhunt started."

Simmer and I were sitting at the very back of the wagon box, our bare feet hanging down. He lay back in the hay and looked up at the puffy clouds in the late afternoon sky.

"Look at the bright side, Kit. Maybe Eddie'll come out and go to picking on us. Then we can get your daddy to shoot him."

Daddy walked hollering around all the barns and sheds but got no reply. Finally, he found Bernie hiding in the chicken house and gave him the legal paper. I didn't know what the paper was about. Probably Bernie's own chicken house wasn't the only one he'd been spending time in.

We reached the train depot in town just at five-thirty, which made us a few minutes early for the five o'clock train. That one was always late.

Bud was already there and loafed around with us until the train came chuffing and squealing into the station. He had brought Rosebud Harlow with him, as he often did. It seemed like half the time you when saw Bud, you saw Rosebud, too.

Rosebud was the six-year-old daughter of Deacon Charles Harlow, our neighbor up the creek. Her real name was Rose Marie but almost nobody but her parents ever called her that. Bud had nicknamed her Rosebud because, he said, he liked the sound of Rose and Bud together. She was a feisty, pig-tailed little tomboy, big-eyed and eager. She could climb a tree as well as any boy her size, and was constantly looking for something new to try. She was always getting hurt and screeching loudly enough to tell the whole county, but it never stopped her from trying the next fool stunt that came to mind. Mrs. Harlow and her grown-up daughter, Miss Mary Ann, said that keeping shoes on Rosebud was like herding cats; try as you might it you just couldn't make it work. But everybody loved her; you couldn't help it.

23

Miss Mary Ann Harlow was Bud Carsons's sweetheart. At least, I reckon that's what you'd call her. He'd been sparking her for a couple of years, and for a while all the old ladies around were wagging their tongues about how it looked like that handsome young Carson boy was about to get his ear notched. But things hadn't gone their way. Bud and Mary Ann were still seeing a lot of each other, but there hadn't been a word about marriage. Now the quilting bees were alive with jabber about how scandalous it was that Bud kept coming to supper at the Harlows' and taking Miss Mary Ann out for buggy rides and still hadn't proposed after all this time.

Miss Mary Ann's parents didn't seem concerned, though. She was several years younger than Bud; she wouldn't get too old for him. They knew him well enough to know that he was a good man and just taking his time about making up his mind to settle down. They seemed confident that he'd pop the question sometime before Mary Ann was too old to give them any grandchildren.

Rosebud seemed to have me in mind for a sweetheart. When she saw Daddy, Simmer and me pull up and jump out of the wagon she came running over and punched me in the belly. Then she hung on my overall pockets and said what she always said.

"Kit, will you be my beau?"

"No, I won't, silly," I said, grabbing her wrists to swing her in a circle. "Baby girls don't need a beau."

I let go of her and she jumped forward to slap me on the arm. "I ain't no baby!" she yelled. Then she aimed a kick at my shin, but I was ready for her and got out of the way. Just then we heard the train whistle and Rosebud forgot about being mad.

"They say you can see the smoke of that train as far away as Butterfield," Simmer observed. "And hear the whistle by the time she gets past Purdy."

I thought maybe he was stretching that one a little bit, but I usually wasn't anywhere around when the train came in, so I really couldn't say.

Finally, the big, sooty cars rattled and scraped to a stop, and the first passenger off was a man in a gray prison officer's uniform. He saw us looking toward him across the platform and when he saw Bud's star, he smiled and stepped toward us, carrying his carpetbag.

We met him halfway and he stuck out his hand toward Bud. "Sheriff Hunt?" he said, friendly-like.

Bud grinned. "No, sir, this is the sheriff." He nodded sideways at my father. Daddy stepped forward a little sheepishly and shook the man's hand. He was always forgetting to pin on his badge.

"I'm Sergeant Lew Jenkins, Missouri Bureau of Prisons." Definitely a friendly type.

"James Hunt, Mr. Jenkins. This is my deputy, Bud Carson. This," he put his hand on my shoulder as if to say he was proud of me, "is my son, Kit. That desperado on th' other side there is Mr. Simmer Downs, his partner in crime. The young lady is Rosebud Harlow, belle of the county."

We had a round of handshakes, and Jenkins took off his hat and bowed to Rosebud. She curtsied back, and I wondered where she'd learned a trick like that.

"Well, Sheriff, thanks for meeting me here on such short notice. I've got a lot to talk to you about as soon as you have time, but first I need to collect my dog from somebody around here."

Bud led the way inside the depot to the baggage counter and Sergeant Jenkins spoke to the harried-looking man in sleeve garters and too much hair grease behind it. The man said, "Yes, sir. Just one minute and I'll meet you out on the platform."

We turned around and headed back out the heavy front doors while the clerk strode hurriedly toward some side entrance and disappeared. A couple of minutes later he came around the corner of the building leading the biggest hound I'd ever seen in my life.

In fact, it would be closer to say the dog was leading him. He had his big head up, snuffing the air as if he had just landed on Mars and couldn't wait to get acquainted with everybody. His huge ears were swinging side to side with every step and he had so much loose skin on his face that he looked like his head had once been twice its size and had shrunk, leaving all that hide sagging. Then he caught wind of Sergeant Jenkins twenty feet away and came towing the poor clerk across the platform like a slow plowboy behind a fast mule. If that dog had had a mile to drag him at that pace, I believe the wind would have whipped the hem out of the man's shirt tail.

You could tell Sergeant Jenkins knew dogs. When that monster got within a few feet of him, wagging and whining and practically dancing on all four feet, Jenkins bent over and started loving him up with hugs and slaps that would have been a pounding to a normal sized dog. A lot of people would have stepped back and reared away from the dog, but he would have just jumped up and put those huge paws on their chest and slapped their face half off with that tongue of his. Jenkins knew that the way to keep a dog from jumping up on you is to go down to him and give him the loving he wants at his level.

The clerk didn't seem to mind turning the dog's leash over to Sergeant Jenkins. In fact, he scooted back inside the depot kind of fast, as if he didn't appreciate the novelty of seeing such a dog. It wasn't every day a dog like this came to Cassville.

Jenkins called him Buck. I wish I had a quarter for every dog I ever heard of that was named Buck. Or every gyp named Lady, for that matter. You'd think people weren't willing to put any thought into something as important as the name that the dog's going to have to listen to every day for the rest of his life. I'm glad my name's not Buck; I'm tired of it already.

But by any name, Buck was a sight for sore eyes. In the first place, he was big. He weighed a hundred and ten pounds if he weighed an ounce, which put him just about twenty pounds heavier than me. His back was as high as the pockets of my overalls, and his nose when he stuck it up to sniff my face very nearly came to my chin. His feet were so big you'd think he could walk on water. His tail was almost too long and skinny for him. But it was his face that got your attention.

As I said before, there was too much face for his head. If he'd stuck his head out a window while the train was on a fast downhill grade, that face would have beaten him to death. The extra yardage was piled up in rows of wrinkles above his eyes that made him look like he was raising his eyebrows in curiosity, except that the eyes themselves sort of drooped all sad-looking, showing the pink underneath the eyeballs. His slobbering jowls hung loose so that he could have breathed in between his side teeth without opening his mouth.

Buck was stocky. At first I thought he was fat, but it wasn't that. He had lots of skin over him, although nothing like on his face, and he was big-boned. Our local hounds tended to be skinny, both because we didn't feed them a whole lot and because they kept the fat run off them. You could usually count the ribs on a hound. Compared to the usual dog, Buck looked too heavy, but after looking at him a minute you saw that he carried his weight with his strength.

His color was interesting, too. He was red, unlike our black and tan coonhounds. But it wasn't a real red red, like a redbone. It was more of a tan, like a black and tan hound with the black patches peeled off. Over all, he was an interesting looking dog. I couldn't wait to see him work.

Sergeant Jenkins was interesting, too. He looked to be about my father's age, late forties or so, with considerably more gray hair. He was stocky and square-shouldered, not tall but straight and starchy-looking. His gray uniform was neat and he wore a shiny black belt with a well-cared-for revolver hanging on it in a holster. He looked like a man who meant business, but his eyes were friendly and it wasn't work for him to smile.

After Buck had had a minute to greet his handler and slobber all over the rest of us, Daddy led the way to the wagon. Bud was staying at the office overnight as he usually did on weekends, so he said goodbye and we headed home in the wagon, Daddy and Mr. Jenkins laughing and talking on the wooden seat like old friends and Simmer and me on the hay in back with Buck, getting acquainted. I had been a little afraid of him at first. You hear so many stories about how bloodhounds are called bloodhounds because they smell the quarry's blood and tear the man all to pieces when they catch him. But Buck was as sweet-natured as a grandma at Christmas time.

When we clattered into the yard an hour later, Bruisin' Susan and the two young dogs bellowed their usual howdies from their pen behind the woodshed. No sooner had we gotten stopped than Buck was over the side and galloping toward our dogs so hard the ground seemed to shake. The two men didn't seem concerned, but Simmer and I followed at a run just in case there was trouble. But we needn't have worried. Hounds are death and judgment on varmints, but they're usually not big on fighting each other. And that's how these dogs acted. They sniffed noses and reared up on the fence to paw at each other, and kept up a barking and howling like there was no tomorrow, but we never heard a growl. Susan and the kids were excited to see a visitor, but not aggravated.

"Old Buck sure is anxious to get acquainted with Susan," Simmer said.

He was right. Buck had barely taken time to give the pups a sniff and hoist a leg against the corner post of their pen before he was rearing up against the wood slat fence around Susan, whining and baying and scratching at the pickets.

"I told you she was in season. If Daddy can find a stud dog with the right blood, we'll have some good puppies to sell around here pretty soon." I leaned down on the board propped diagonally against Susan's gate to wedge it in tighter. I'd have to keep Buck away from her or I might end up with a batch of pups that didn't know whether to chase varmints or people.

I reached over the fence to give Susan a quick pat, then picked up Buck's leash where it was dragging on the ground and, with a little help from Simmer, dragged him around to the front porch where Daddy was introducing Sergeant Jenkins to my mother.

"Not in the least, Mr. Jenkins," she was saying. "We've got plenty of room and it's no trouble at all to have you for a few days. Company will be a welcome change."

Jenkins had his hat in his hand. He knew how to talk to ladies. "Well, I certainly thank you, Mrs. Hunt. It'll be a great help to be here where I can coordinate things with your husband once we get a lead on our man."

Then Mama was shooing all of us inside for supper, and Simmer and I tied Buck to the walnut tree in the yard before going in. That evening after the sun went down, we all collected out front, grown-ups on the porch and Simmer and me on the grass. He and I had made a run to his house to get permission for him to stay overnight with me so we could see what was going to happen about the manhunt.

I've always loved that time of day in the summer. You can sit outdoors and you're not too cold and not too hot. There are a few mosquitoes, but you can keep a smoky fire going in a smudge pot and that'll clear out most of them. It gets all quiet in the early evening and from our front porch you begin to notice you can hear the creek running down yonder across the pasture. The whippoorwills began to call, thin blankets of fog appear in layers across the creek bottom, the bullfrogs start tuning up their deep bass *chuggarump!* while the crickets and little tree frogs practice their soprano. The sun has been down for a while already, and the blue of the sky becomes dark blue as the stars begin to appear. There's still a faint rosy glow where

30

the sun said goodnight before going to bed over the hills at the west end of the valley. A summer evening like that always made me feel sorry for everybody who doesn't live in the Ozark hills of Missouri.

Tonight was even better than usual because Simmer and I got to listen to Daddy and Sergeant Jenkins talk business. Jenkins, it turned out, was just as patient as my father when it came to answering boys' questions, even when they had a lot of them. We made good use of their patience, too.

"So tell me," my father was saying, "who is this feller that escaped and what's he all about? Is he a dangerous type?"

Jenkins twisted beside him on the porch swing and pulled a pipe and pouch of tobacco from his pocket. A moment later a match flared, highlighting his rugged face in its glow. I was glad he couldn't see my mother's face just then. I knew what she thought of smoking.

"No," he answered my father. "He's not one we'd normally be concerned about as far as that goes, not in prison for violent crime. He's been a pretty compliant inmate in the nine months we've had him at Springfield. 'Course, any of 'em can get mean when they're desperate, but it's not like he's a cold-blooded killer. The reason we're going to such lengths to get him back is not that he's such a menace to the public safety, but because we need him. He's got important information."

Simmer and I sat very still on the grass. If the adults would forget we were there, the chances were much greater that they'd say something really interesting.

"Information? Like court evidence or like something to help an investigation?" my father queried.

"Both, in fact. This man – his name is Charles Burton, by the way – was arrested in St. Louis for fraud. That was about a year ago. Since then we've arrested two other men who were involved in the scheme with him, and we think there's several more. Pretty big ring. So we need his testimony against the suspects we have in custody, and we also need information from him on the others involved. Of course, he's not too excited about helping us, even though it might make us go easier on him. His friends wouldn't appreciate his giving information about them, and they might try to do something about it. So he thought he'd be better off trying his luck in the woods than waiting for his friends to catch up to him or for us to find a way to get information out of him that would make him more enemies. He saw a chance to escape from a work detail one day, and he took it. Guard saw him go, but fired a second too late. Burton was in the woods."

My father swung in silence a moment. "What makes you think he's headed this way? Springfield's a good ways from here."

"We've got circulars and posters out on him. He's been loose for a week and there's been some reports of sightings. A couple of them, which were pretty authentic-sounding, put him moving this way, and besides it's right on the way to Indian Territory, which is as good a place for a fugitive to hide as any. So the main office sent Buck and me down here to be handier if another citizen spots him. And I expect somebody will. Burton is city-bred. Not the type to live off the land. He'll risk approaching somebody's house for food, counting on them not having heard about him, or he'll raid some gardens or chicken houses. When you get the word, Buck will be ready to follow up on it." The glow of his pipe brightened as he took a pull on it.

I had been patient so far, sitting there in the almost-dark waiting for the men to start talking dogs. Simmer and I were off to the side of the porch, patting Buck who was tied to the tree by his long leather strap. We had compromised between wanting to mess with him and wanting to hear the conversation on the porch. Buck had stretched his strap to the limit to get some petting, so we were able to satisfy him and ourselves, too. Finally, my father asked a question that was worthwhile.

"Tell me about your bloodhounds, Lew. How do you work 'em?"

All of a sudden Simmer and I stopped rubbing on Buck, which was just as well. We'd probably about worn the hair off him already. We perked up our ears.

"Well, it's right much different than folks think if all they know about 'em is what they've read in stories. Before we got dogs at the prison, I always thought they ran 'em in packs of three or four dogs, like coonhounds, and several men probably followed 'em on horseback. But I found out that wasn't the way a-tall. You take one dog, like old Buck here, and you hook that long leather strap on him and you just be ready to go through whatever he goes through. You've got to stay hitched to him, because if he ever gets loose, he's gone on after his man and he don't look back."

"You can't just follow his barking and head him off?"

"A bloodhound don't bark on trail. 'Least, the purebred ones don't."

I felt my mouth drop open in astonishment. All the dime novels had the desperadoes panicking at the sound of the hounds baying behind them, getting closer and closer.

There were some coon dogs that trailed silent, but they were usually mixed breeds. They were useless unless hunted with other dogs so you could find them when they treed a coon. I wouldn't have wanted one because I wanted me and my dog to be able to hunt alone.

"Is that right?" my father said, wonderingly. "I hadn't never thought of that, but I reckon it's the only way. It wouldn't do to let your man know exactly where you are all the time. Give him time to circle a bluff and come back over the top to drop a rock on your head as you went by on his track."

"You can forget doing all your hunting on horseback, too. Where an escaped convict's headed is places no horse can go. Besides, there's so many fences around the country you'd lose a lot of time looking for gates, or having to pull staples to drop wire so the horses could step over. You need a man on the strap to handle the dog and another man to carry a shotgun. The dog man can carry a pistol, but he can't manage a dog and a long gun both in the woods. 'Sides, he can't watch the dog, look for visual sign, and watch for the bad man all at the same time. Then it's all right to have some extra men on horseback, long as they stay well behind the dog so they don't trash up the scent where the man's pulled a loop or circle or something."

Finally, I just had to interrupt and say something. "What kind of tricks can they pull to throw the dog off?" I asked, getting up from the ground and moving to the porch steps. Simmer stayed to give Buck a farewell pat, then followed me.

"Well, there's lots of things he can do to slow the dog down. It's pretty hard to throw one off altogether, but a man can buy himself some time. Like running into an old barn or house, or a cave if he can find one. If he goes in, stomps around a little to stink the place up with his scent, then runs out on the same track and jumps off at an angle, the dog man has to check out the building to see if the man is still in there. So you tie your dog up and search the place, or wait until your riders can catch up and go through it for you. While you're wasting time there, your escapee is making tracks in another direction.

"Another thing a man can do is to go straight downhill into a tight holler. Then he runs around in circles and crisscrosses his own tracks to leave a heavy concentration of scent and leaves by a path that won't hold a scent good, like if there's a gravel wash in the middle of the holler. There's more to smell in the leaves and bushes than on that little trail of gravel, so it takes the dog a while to decide that's the way he went. And 'course there's cricks, which mess up a dog if there's enough water and not a lot of overhanging brush to hold scent."

This was the kind of talk I loved. I had done enough hunting to know some of the tricks coons could use to throw dogs off and it was amazing what they knew. One big old boar coon we chased got onto a deer track and followed it by scent like a hound for half a mile, then swam down a crick the deer had jumped. Bruisin' Susan had finally figured out what had happened and went off downstream and picked up the coon track where it had left the water. But the two young dogs had gotten it into their heads that wherever that deer was going was where they'd find the coon. They didn't get home until dinner time the next day.

I didn't have to say much more, which was a good thing because my folks didn't like kids to be always interrupting adult company. But Daddy and Mr. Jenkins had got the pump primed and got to swapping dog and manhunt stories at a gallop that lasted a good long time. Their talk ranged so far and wide that I can't remember every story they told or every interesting fact they brought up that I hadn't heard before and wanted to hang onto. But one thing that stuck in my head was that Buck, coming to the prison as a grown and trained dog of quality bloodlines, had cost the state a hundred and fifty dollars. That was more than Bud Carson had paid for his high-stepping horse! I almost couldn't believe it.

Mama finally made Simmer and me go up to bed, but we'd heard enough to give us something to talk about for a while. It must have been long after midnight when we drifted off to sleep, but we were still the first ones up and out the door. And when we stood on the porch in the early morning sun and saw what had happened, we just about lay down and died.

Chapter 4

RUNAWAY DOGS

Buck was gone. Sergeant Jenkins had said he was going to leave him tied to the tree where he'd been the evening before, and there was the bucket of water Simmer and I had brought for him. The leather leash was still tied to the fence, too, but it had been chewed off clean as a whistle at Buck's end and now lay stretched across the yard and covered with dew as if it had been lying there still for quite a while. The dew covered the grass, too, in a shiny, even blanket so you could see it had been hours since Buck had disturbed it.

Simmer and I just stared at the chewed-off strap and then at each other. I guessed he felt the same as I did, and that was pretty puny.

"Oh, mercy, Kit! You reckon we ought to wake up your folks and Mr. Jenkins?"

I thought a minute. "Let's have a look around ourselves first. No sense bothering them if we can help it." He agreed because neither of us was eager to bring the news to the grownups.

Simmer and I weren't the fussy type who waste time getting in and out of clothes just for sleep, at least in the summer, so we didn't have to waste any time getting started. The thought hit both of us at once that the first place to look was around our dog pen. Dogs like company, so Buck might just have gone back there to spend the night with friends. But when we came around the corner of the woodshed, not only was Buck not there, but Bruisin' Susan wasn't either. Those two had eloped.

Simmer and I exchanged another panicked look. "Kit," he said, "I'd say your daddy ain't gonna need that good coon dog stud he was lookin' for."

"No, I reckon he ain't." I stood leaning on the slat gate of Susan's pen, trying to take it all in. We had lost Sergeant Jenkins' prize bloodhound and Daddy's champion coon dog in one night's time. If Buck followed Susan on some coon track, they might not make it back before tomorrow, which would be awful if somebody spotted that Burton fellow today. And surely, undoubtedly, Susan was going to present my father with a batch of pups that would be half coon dog and half man dog. What if you couldn't break a pup like that to specialize in one or the other? There was no use for a man dog that would chase coons or a coon dog that would chase men. It looked like my dream of having my very own coon dog pup to train was dead as a hammer. What if some of the pups wanted to chase coons but didn't bark on track? I shoved the thought away from me. There were too many different things to worry about. We'd have to work on getting the dogs back first and take the rest when it came.

We went back to the house in a hurry and woke Daddy, who woke Sergeant Jenkins. Pretty soon they both came clumping out on the front porch in their boots. They weren't happy, but at least they weren't mad at Simmer and me.

"Doggone it, Lew, I wish I'd thought. My black and tan gyp's in season and I should have put your dog in a pen so he couldn't just chew loose," my father was saying.

"No, James, that wouldn't have made any difference. That Buck dog is the biggest escape artist in the country. He'll climb out of any fence you put him in. Up at the prison we had to build a kennel with a top over it to stop his climbing. Then he started digging out so we had to lay fence wire underneath it, too. It's the beatingest thing you ever seen."

They both tried a holler or two from up on the porch, Daddy yelling for Susan and then Jenkins taking a turn shouting at Buck. But all of us knew it wouldn't do any good. Those dogs were out somewhere playing in the woods and they weren't going to cut their vacation short for any of us.

They gave up the hollering pretty quick and followed Simmer and me around back to the dog pens. Blackie and Slick, the two young hounds, bayed us a loud good morning but Susan's pen was deserted.

My father started to speak, or rather yell, to make himself heard above Slick and Blackie. "Well, there's what hap—Shut up, you two!" It is right frazzling, trying to talk over the continual baying of two big hound dogs. But they shut up when Daddy used his sheriff volume. It would shrivel up any dog, and Bud says that more than once he's seen Daddy use that voice to stop a fleeing suspect without ever pulling his pistol. He never used it at me, not close up anyway, but you can bet I'd have listened to him.

39

"There's what happened. Buck knocked the prop away from the gate."

We looked. Sure enough, the weathered piece of board that was usually wedged in the ground at one end and against the gate at the other, had been knocked away. In my mind I could just see Buck running back and forth outside the fence looking for a hole to get through. A big old horse like him wouldn't have to any more than brush against that prop to knock it out of the way and let the gate swing open. Evidently he had run right smack into it, because now it was lying four feet to the side of where it had been.

"Well, if that don't beat all." Sergeant Jenkins took off his hat and scratched his head, then turned to my father. "Well, James, where you reckon is the best place to start looking?"

Daddy spoke to me. "Kit, go saddle Chip and Ribbon. Then you boys take off up the holler behind the house here and Mr. Jenkins and me'll go up and down the road. Let's all take a pistol and fire off three shots in the air if we find 'em. If we ain't found 'em in a couple o' hours, we'll meet back here and try something else."

It didn't take five minutes for Simmer and me to get the horses saddled and my .22 revolver from the house. Then Sergeant Jenkins rode Ribbon up the road toward town, hollering "Buck! Here, Buck!" while Daddy trotted his buckskin Chip down toward Star City, stopping every so often to blow on the twisted, carved goat's horn he used to call his coon dogs. Simmer and I headed up the hollow back of our house and up the side of the hill beyond. There was a dead tree up there that you could climb and see all the way up the creek for a mile or more. I thought I'd get Simmer to boost me up to the lowest limb and have a look.

We ran and hollered and hollered and ran, knowing all the time that it wasn't likely those two dogs would come to us unless we got within sight of them. It was Sunday morning, but this little complication meant no church for me today. Daddy had let me help out with some sheriffing situations before and I knew that this job was important enough that it had to be done right now.

I couldn't see any sign of the dogs from the top of the dead tree, though the morning was clear and bright. When I came sliding down the trunk, scattering a shower of bark and rotten wood, Simmer was starting to calm down. He always was good at calming down.

"Well, what's next?" he asked me.

I thought a minute. "Well, I guess there's not much point in splitting up. If you found 'em, they probably wouldn't let you catch 'em, since neither of 'em belongs to you. Let's head back over the ridge here and see if we have any luck."

So we did, but the only luck we had was the wrong kind. We were already a little winded when we met the men back at the house and learned that Daddy and Jenkins hadn't done any better. We ate a quick breakfast of ham and eggs, then headed out to look in different directions. Simmer and I walked and hollered until we got to wishing we hadn't ever seen a dog in our lives. When we finally came back to the house about four in the afternoon, the men were already there. They had just arrived to find Buck and Susan there ahead of them. Mama said they had come back on their own and scratched at the door for something to eat. She had put Susan back in her pen and tied Buck to the tree where he had been before, only this time she used a trace chain hooked to his collar.

As Simmer and I got close to the house we could see that Buck was out front again and you can bet we were relieved to hear his big Owoo-woo-woo welcoming us home. We could also see my father hitching Henry and Henrietta to the wagon again and we wondered what that was all about. We found out as soon as he saw us coming.

"Hurry it up, boys! Bud's just been here and said somebody's seen this escaped convict. We got us a chase!"

Chapter 5

THE MANHUNT

Chip and Ribbon were tired after hunting dogs all day, so we didn't even take them. Daddy just dumped their saddles in the back of the wagon along with his rifle and other manhunting gear.

"We can borrow saddlehorses, if we need 'em, from farmers along the way," he said. Everybody knew him because he was the sheriff and anybody would be glad to loan him saddle stock because they knew the animals would be looked after.

Simmer and I didn't hesitate but jumped right in the back of the wagon. Daddy stepped up and sat on the seat, gathering up the lines as if he was in a hurry, which he was. Sergeant Jenkins came out of the house at a trot, strapping his pistol belt on as he came. As he was untying Buck from the fence Mama hurried out the front door, slamming the screen behind her, for which she would have scolded me if I'd done it. Mama always got nervous when Daddy was on a chase. She handed a cloth flour sack up to Daddy. The sack was stuffed so that I hoped it was vittles. Buck hoped so too, and shoved his big head over Daddy's shoulder to investigate, slobbering all over him in the process.

"Get back, dog!" shouted Jenkins, giving him a shove. Simmer and I scrambled to get hold on his tie chain and pull him back out of Daddy's way, but Daddy just grinned, leaned over to give Mama a kiss and started backing the horses out into the road. Then he slapped the lines on the horses' backs and they started off, giving the wagon a jerk that made it all of a sudden easy for us to pull Buck back. It was a little too easy in fact, because since we were already hauling back on his chain with all our strength the jerk was all he needed to do a neat roll and land in our laps. Away we went, scattering gravel from under the wheels and wrestling that big hound dog in the hay.

Simmer and I got set after a minute and tied Buck off short so he couldn't trample us. I was so excited I couldn't hold it in. I leaned 'way over to Simmer and let the rattle of the wagon cover my voice up where nobody would hear me but him.

"Sim! Can you believe this? We're gettin' to go on a real manhunt—just like the Texas Rangers!"

Even Simmer couldn't help being het up about this. "Oh, ain't it grand! I thought sure your mama would stop us and make us get out of the wagon."

"So did I," I told him over the clatter. "I reckon she was so rattled by losing the dogs and then Bud coming and Daddy not being back and then having to get us ready to go so quick that she forgot she was supposed to make a fuss."

Right then Simmer and I would have jumped up and started dancing if we hadn't been in the back of a jolting wagon with a horse-sized dog scrambling around. When we were both excited about something we'd kind of

44

automatically go to doing our Official Indian War Dance. We didn't know just how Indians did it, but our version was to come out with a long yell, smack each other's palms, then strike our forearms together, then hop around each other in sort of a circle, yelling and screeching and shaking our fists in the air. Usually we ended it by hanging on each other and laughing about how silly we must look. It was just one of those fun things that boys invent to do.

"Do you think your pa will let us go with him and Mr. Jenkins and Buck?"

"I doubt it. That's the kind of stuff grown folks are always saying is too dangerous for kids. But it'll be fun just to be along for the ride."

And it was fun. It was fun just feeling the tickle of the jitters in our bellies as we thought about going on a real manhunt. We rode along in the late afternoon sunshine, bouncing comfortably on the hay and patting Buck when we took a notion. Bud, who had been going around rousting out some men to form a posse, met us before we got to town and rode beside us on his spirited horse with his spurs jingling and the warm spring wind blowing his shirt collar open. He grinned at me and Simmer once like he knew just what we were thinking. I believe he was glad, too, that we had been given a chance to get in on some real lawman action instead of being left at home like the women and babies.

It was almost six when we pulled up at the farm of Jonas Schrum, several miles east of town. The place was crowded with wagons and men on horseback. You could always get a crowd out for posse duty. It didn't happen often, but when a manhunt came it was a bigger occasion than a hog slaughtering. Word got around quick and all the local men and older boys showed up on foot and horseback to help out. Daddy said that a lot of the men were more company than help, but he hated to send any of them away because that made them mad and then you might have trouble getting enough help next time.

Despite the time, the sun was still high and the day warm. As we rolled in to the barnyard we saw men gathered in bunches smoking and talking, mostly under the shade of the yard trees. Everybody looked up when they heard it was the sheriff and the bloodhound man coming. Those who were squatting or leaning on fences stood up and everybody started toward us as the wagon stopped and Daddy set the brake. Mr. Schrum stepped between men and walked up to my father.

"Howdy, James," he said, his hands inside his overall bib. He was a tall, lanky man of about fifty or sixty with a big Adam's apple and a shadow of salt-and-pepper whiskers he never seemed to be without.

"Howdy, Jonas. You caught him yet?"

Several of the men chuckled. Most of them were looking with interest at Buck.

"No, but at least I seen him. That's more'n anybody else can say." He said everything with such a straight face that you almost didn't know when he was playing. He was something like Simmer.

Daddy introduced Sergeant Jenkins to the men gathered around then asked Mr. Schrum a few questions. Mr. Schrum told him about coming out at dawn to do the chores and hearing a ruckus in the chicken house. He had thought a possum had gotten in and was snatching a hen, but then he noticed that the chicken house door was wide open. Only a two-legged varmint could have done that.

46

Just as he turned and headed back into the house to get his shotgun, a man ran out of the chicken house with a hat full of eggs. He tore out around back, keeping the chicken house between him and Mr. Schrum's shotgun, and made it across the pasture and into the woods before Mr. Schrum could get into and out of the house.

"Did you walk out and look for him in the woods?" Daddy asked him.

"Nope. I was in town yesterday evenin' and heered that there dog was here. So, when I thought about my egg thief maybe bein' your convict, I stayed out of that field and kep' ever'body else out, too, so the track wouldn't get trashed up with somebody else's smell."

Sergeant Jenkins seemed surprised. "Well now, that's more sense than a whole lot of lawmen show. Half the time I get on the scene of a robbery or break-in and the deputies have tracked all over creation looking for the man, when he's probably miles away. Then I have to take my dog in and try to make something out of a mess like that. You'd think if they want us to come loan them our dog they'd take some kind of care of the crime scene, but a lot of the time they don't."

"Most folks around here have hounds," Daddy told him. "Maybe they're a little more likely than some people to know how a dog works."

Sergeant Jenkins asked Mr. Schrum for a description of the man he had seen. It sounded like Burton.

"Was he wearing stripes?" Jenkins asked.

"No, he had on reg'lar clothes, just like me." That could have been pretty shabby. Mr. Schrum didn't dress up much.

47

Mr. Jenkins and my father looked at each other. "Wouldn't be hard to grab some clothes off the line somewhere," Jenkins said.

My father nodded thoughtfully. "Want to give it a try?"

"Yeah, let's try it." The prison officer looked tired already, which considering all the riding and hollering he'd done today, didn't surprise me. But Simmer and I had more than gotten our second wind riding in the wagon and our nerves tingled to get in on the hunt.

"All right, men," my father was saying. "I'm gonna go with Sergeant Jenkins and the dog on foot. Anybody else that wants to come along can, but only on horseback so we don't get too much man smell scattered around on the ground and make it hard for the dog. Stay well behind us all the time. If we go in woods where you can't see us, for Pete's sake don't shoot at anything. I expect the man'll stay in the brush where the horses can't get to, but if you stay in hollering distance you can come running if we need help."

He looked around at the group as if waiting to see if anybody had any questions. None of the twenty or so men said anything.

"Now I need two horses for my boys here," Daddy said, nodding toward me and Simmer. "Can anybody help me out?"

Nobody moved for a minute. Then Lloyd Snodgrass, Mr. Schrum's neighbor down the road, spoke up. "Here, one of 'em can take my horse. I don't care that much about goin' long as you've got plenty of help, James. I'll walk on back to the house and do my chores."

"I've got my boy's pony out back," said Mr. Schrum. "He ain't big, but he'll do fer the little feller, there." He was looking at me. There wasn't a bit of meanness meant by it, but he might as well have stomped on my toe as call me the little feller. Oh, well, I'd been called worse than that, and at least I had a horse to ride.

We all mounted while Jenkins got Buck down from the wagon and rigged him up. I expected him to just tie a rope on the dog's collar, but that wasn't what happened. He picked up something that looked like a horse halter from the back of the wagon and went to strapping it around Buck's chest and barrel. I saw that it was some kind of a harness. It had an iron ring on it that rode right up on the middle of the dog's back. I guessed that the rope or leash would be hooked to that. I found out I was right a minute later because Jenkins reached into the wagon box again and brought out Buck's long leather strap. I saw it had been stuck back together with some of Daddy's copper rivets that he kept for mending horse harness and such. Jenkins snapped the end of the leash into the ring and you could just see Buck come alive. He had been dancing ever since his boss had brought out the harness and started putting it on him. But when he heard the metallic snap of the clip on that leash, he lunged forward so hard that men stepped out of his way.

Sergeant Jenkins guided him out the gate into the pasture behind the chicken house. I heard a man ask, "Don't he need somethin' with the feller's smell on it?" And I knew the answer. Buck would follow the first man track he struck and stay on it unless he struck a fresher one. It was just like a coon dog; he just wants coon and he doesn't care which one. I wondered, though, what you did when your suspect was running through town or someplace where there were other people. I'd have to remember to ask Sergeant Jenkins that.

Sure enough, Buck was a silent tracker. Not only did he not raise his head and bay, he didn't raise his head at all. He saw what direction Jenkins wanted him to go, then stuck his big nose to the grass and went to dragging the man along behind him. Simmer and I, being boys, pushed ahead of the other riders to watch Buck. It was only a couple hundred yards to the woods, but before we got there I saw why tracking dogs are harnessed the way they are.

The track was now twelve or thirteen hours old and Buck was having to dig to get it. He wasn't trotting in a straight line, but swinging left and right, anxiously snuffing all around. He had the awkward-looking trot of a hound, the hindquarters never quite lined up with the front legs as if the rear end wasn't sure the front end knew where it was going. Sometimes he'd even turn a circle and step over the leash. When he did that the strap would look like it was just about to get all tangled around Buck and maybe hogtie him. But each time, he'd step right out of the tangle with his hind legs—his front legs hadn't ever been in any danger—and leave it behind to straighten out when he pulled the strap taut again. Now I knew. Everybody's seen a tied dog get loose and run off dragging his chain. Hooked to his collar, the weight of the chain pulls down so that the collar slips around and the ring is on the bottom of his neck. A few more steps and the dog is dragging the chain between his legs, getting tangled in it and stepping on it with his hind feet until it drives him to distraction. That never happened to Buck. Once in a while he'd get a hind leg over the strap, but when he did he'd hike that leg up and go a pace or two on three legs. The strap would pull itself up and out and be all above and behind him. It was a neat trick.

I also figured out quickly why the strap was so long. Buck wasn't waiting on anybody, so if Sergeant Jenkins didn't want to go through every thicket and blackberry patch Buck did, he had to drop the leash and run around to the other side. A couple of times, Buck got out before his boss got around and would have been gone if there hadn't been fifteen feet of strap behind him for Jenkins to catch as it slid by.

It was easy to see when Buck hit the main trail. He had at first been weaving back and forth and all around, although moving in the same general direction all the time. That meant it was a cold trail and the scent was scattered. But suddenly he took a sharp turn to the left and started pulling Sergeant Jenkins much faster and more confidently toward the woods. There was a lot of cow smell in the pasture, and I wondered how much that would cloud things up for Buck. It doesn't help coon hounds any.

Then they were at the barbed wire fence at the edge of the pasture and I knew Buck was right. No cow had gone through that fence. He never hesitated a minute; he got down on his belly and started to crawl under. The top of his harness caught for a minute on the wire but Jenkins seemed to be expecting that and quickly jerked up on the wire, unhooking it. Then he handed the leash to my father, who snubbed it around the nearest post while Jenkins crawled through the fence. My father then handed the end of the strap over the fence to Jenkins. He took the strap and Daddy's gun while Daddy crawled through.

Buck saw no need to wait on the slower members of the pack, and kept lunging against the strap the whole time. When they were finally ready to go on, he took off through the woods at a gallop. Without the cow smell, and with the

51

carpet of leaves to keep the ground moist and hold the scent, the woods make for an easy track. Buck went charging off through the woods just plowing the leaves. Now I saw why bloodhounds are big. The handler can't keep up on his own steam and ends up being dragged part of the time. A little dog would wear down quicker than a hoss like Buck. It struck me again what a disadvantage it is to be little.

I didn't see much of the rest of the chase. It was a still evening, so we heard a lot of sticks popping as they were stepped on and the thrashing of two men and a dog through the dry leaves. Sergeant Jenkins' voice floated back to us, praising and encouraging his dog. But we couldn't get our horses through the fence, and so we had to leave the Schrum place and ride down the road to the south listening for the dog men and watching out in case they flushed Burton out in the open. Sometimes they would come close and we could hear them plainly, Jenkins encouraging Buck with words we could make out clear as if he was standing right beside us. Then other times the sound would fade and we heard nothing at all. Once in a while the brush would thin out and we could ride out in the woods a ways, and once it got us close enough to hear that they were still going south. Mostly we just stayed on the road and heard snatches of noise now and then. We didn't see any sign of Burton, if it was him, though I watched the side of the road carefully for tracks.

The sun was beginning to get low and it was dusky on the road because of the woods on both sides. Little needlepoints of sunlight shooting horizontally through the trees said sundown was upon us. We had been out almost three hours and hadn't heard anything for the last hour. We had stopped drifting aimlessly down the road and watered our horses where a crystal clear spring branch crossed it. Simmer edged his horse up beside me.

"You reckon they're doing any good, Kit?" he asked. I knew he was getting bored. So was I.

Just as I opened my mouth to answer him, Mr. Schrum came loping up to the rear of the group. I hadn't realized he had been lagging behind.

"Come on, boys, I jest heered 'em! They're a-headin' toward the road back up a ways!" He wasn't exactly excited, but he was as close to it as I'd think he ever got. We all wheeled our horses, those of us that were in the saddle, and lit out the way we had come. Those who had dismounted and were standing talking or tossing pebbles in the stream jumped toward their horses, cussing and fumbling and generally making the horses so nervous they shied away and could hardly be mounted at all.

Simmer and I did our best, but we couldn't move up in the pack much because the others had a head start and the road was narrow to pass. My pony wouldn't have been fast enough to pass anybody anyway, hardly. But it was a great feeling, riding along with a real posse in the dusky woods with the hooves pounding and bits of gravel flying up and hitting us. I looked sideways once at Simmer and I hardly knew him. I'd never seen his eyes so wide open.

We must have gone about a half a mile when the leaders started slowing down. We found ourselves at the top of a steep hill behind Mr. Schrum, who had been in the lead turning back, and Bud, who had the fastest horse. Finally, everybody caught up and stood still. Even over the blowing and stomping of the horses, you could hear it.

Men walking through dry leaves. Occasionally a stick cracking as it was stepped on.

Bud led us down the other side of the hill and the noise came closer. I had the feeling they were on the other side of a low ridge from us. It was almost completely dark down here. Bud cupped a hand beside his mouth and hollered.

"Halloooo!"

They waited a minute for the echo to die, then I heard my father's big voice.

"We're a-comin'!"

Then it was quiet again except for the thrashing of their footsteps in the leaves. After a few minutes Daddy yelled again. He seemed to be looking for direction.

"Over here!" called Bud. The rest of us sat as still as we could, but it wasn't necessary. You could hear them plain as day now, and I could have sworn there was enough noise for three men and a dog. Not five minutes later, three tall shadows and a low one stepped out of the bushes onto the dark road.

Chapter 6

RUNT OF THE LITTER

Granny James sure was right when she said that God works in strange ways. I never would have believed some of the things that happened the rest of that summer.

For the first month or so after the manhunt, Simmer and I went to town every chance we got. Of course everybody had heard about us getting to go along, and weren't the boys all jealous! Oh, they all scoffed and said how it wasn't nothing, that we hadn't even gotten to go in the woods with Buck. There were more than the usual comments about how I was so puny I had to stand twice to make a shadow. But we knew, Simmer and me, that they were all dying inside. They felt cheated out of the chance of a lifetime.

We even got our names in the paper. Not that that's so hard to do, not in a town that's so slow for news that you get written up for having relatives come to visit from Arkansas. But this was a great big story with follow-up pieces in later editions. Still, that was nothing to the way the tale got more colorful every time Simmer or I told it.

And others told it too. It grew and developed, got deeper and darker and more dangerous until I hardly recognized it as the same trip I'd been on. But I would never dampen anybody's pleasure by setting the record absolutely straight. After all, who was I to claim I remembered every detail?

It was a sight to behold, how folks did go on. Every time you heard the latest version, the criminal was more dangerous, there were more men in the posse, there was a bigger fight at the capture, the chase went on for more miles. And the track was a couple of hours older.

That's why we got so much money for Bruisin' Susan's pups. Word got around that Buck was their pappy, and pretty soon all the men were speculating as to what sort of dogs they'd be. Buck's fame had spread far and wide because he tracked and caught a man on a trail that had been day-old when he started. And had done it in less than three hours, and the man with that much of a headstart. It almost seemed impossible to them, but Sergeant Jenkins explained it to Simmer and me before he went back to Springfield.

"The only hard part was sorting out Burton's track from all the cow scent in the pasture. Once we got into the woods, the leaves on the ground had held plenty of scent. And Burton, being a city boy, had no notion of how to hide his trail. Besides, the man had been on the run for nearly a week. He was exhausted and just about starved to death. He stopped that morning as soon as he made sure Mr. Schrum wasn't following him. He spent most of the day sleeping in a thicket, then moved on again late in the afternoon. So you see, most of the track Buck followed had was only a couple of hours old. That's an easy trick for a dog like Buck in the woods."

But his fame grew anyway. Arnold Wilson, the town barber, did his share. He loved a story that pleased his customers, believing as he did that part of a barber's sacred trust is to entertain people as well as making them look better. Considering the hair restorer on his shelves and the shiny nakedness of his scalp, you'd have thought people would think twice before believing him. But you know how people are.

Within two weeks, Buck had a whole pedigree and life history that would have dumfounded Sergeant Jenkins. Buck was descended from a centuries-long line of famous English hounds originally bred by King Louis the XIV. Mama said she didn't know how they believed that one, since King Louis was French. I reckon they just didn't think of it. Buck had done some wonderful things in his own right, too. He had caught over seven hundred criminals, one of them a desperate outlaw that he chased for a thousand miles through trackless desert. The trail had been a week old when he had struck it.

The Bureau of Prisons had paid ten thousand dollars for him.

Mama was pretty disgusted with all the gossip, but Daddy and Bud and Simmer and I all thought it was a great joke. At first we egged it on a little, but then we decided it would be more fun to see how far it went all by itself. So we just clammed up and listened to see what the latest version of the story had to say.

A mama dog carries pups about sixty days, so that's how I remember about when the first person asked about buying one of Susan's babies. It was Moe Benner, one of the men who had been on the posse. He came sidling up to Daddy on the boardwalk in town one day, looking so relaxed and careless that Daddy knew he had something on his mind. He soon found out what it was.

"Say, James, did your old gyp ever have them pups?" This came after several remarks on the weather failed to engage my father very much in the conversation.

"No, Moe, she ain't had 'em yet. Be a week or so. But I'll shore be interested to see 'em when they get here."

Moe had pulled out his knife and gone to carving tobacco from a plug to stuff his pipe. "Reckon them dogs'll be any good, seein's how their breedin's kinda mixed up?" He put a match to his pipe and puffed a time or two to get it going, leaning on the other side of the store porch column Daddy was holding up.

My father spread a lazy smile over his face and looked around as if Main Street was fascinating and this conversation was just an afterthought. "Oh, I don't see how they could help bein' good. With the bloodlines they get from both sides, an' all."

"Wal, I mean for coon huntin' in partickler, you know. What with that ugly old daddy dog bein' a silent tracker an' all, and the pups bein' out of two kinds of dog. Coon dog wouldn't be worth mu- I mean, wouldn't be much good if it wouldn't bark on a track or wanted to go off a-huntin' people."

Daddy just smiled again and heaved his shoulder off the post.

"Aw, I 'spect that can be worked out," he said, and walked off down the boardwalk.

He set a price on those pups that was three times what any of them were worth and could have sold twice as many as the seven that Bruisin' Susan had.

I was so tickled when they finally came, that August, that I didn't know what to do with myself. I had thought those puppies would be worthless mongrels, hard to find takers for. Instead, everybody and his brother wanted one. Once their eyes were open, I used to go out every day and let them out of the pen. Simmer would come over and we would lay down on the grass and let them romp all over us. Simmer brought his little brother Bobby over, too. Bobby was six and a real pistol. He had always tagged along after us, wanting to do everything we did whether he was big enough or not. He loved those pups, too, and was all the time begging Simmer to come over to our place and play with them. His favorite one was the runt.

Most litters have one pup that's smaller than the rest. A lot of times it doesn't start out being so very puny, far as you can tell, but it keeps getting crowded away from the milk pipe and then doesn't grow as fast as the others. By weaning time at six weeks, he may be way behind all the others and will probably never catch up. I think that's why our runt didn't get sold at first.

Men came to the house before the pups were halfway weaning age, watching them, looking in their mouths, wallowing them around every which away and finally tying a piece of colored yarn around the neck of their pick so nobody else would get it. When a prospective buyer came, Daddy would take him around to the dog pen and then make some excuse to step into the house for a minute. Then he'd watch, grinning, from the kitchen window as the man sorted through the pups.

"I'm pretty sure some of those strings got switched from dog to dog," he chuckled. "Matter of fact, I thought I saw a wad of several different colors of yarn sticking out of Moe Benner's back pocket when he came."

But he knew it was far too early to tell anything much about a pup anyway, and most of them looked so much alike that nobody ever noticed.

Daddy wouldn't let any of the pups go before they were eight weeks old. Most people sell them by six if not before, because they're weaned from Mama and they can eat solid food. But Daddy felt like it made them happier somehow to stay with their mother longer. He had always said that, but this time I suspected he was enjoying the misery of all those men who were waiting on their pups, not knowing whether they would even hunt coons a day in their lives, but scared to death somebody else was going to cheat them out of their pick.

Still nobody picked the runt, so he was left when the others all went to their new homes. Bobby kept coming over as often as he could to play with him, and I wasn't all that anxious to let him go, myself. I loved having a puppy around just because they're so full of fun and devilment. I could sit for hours and watch puppies play.

But it never entered my mind to keep Runt permanently. Never mind that every coon hunter in the country was slobbering to get one of Buck's and Bruisin' Susan's pups, I wasn't interested. I felt like all my life everything I had was second-rate stuff. I wanted a repeating rifle and mine was a single shot. I wanted a horse of my own, a horse like Bud's, and all I had to ride was Chip or Ribbon, my parents' horses. And the thing I felt worst about was myself. I was a runt, just as sure as that puppy was. I had always done everything I could to make up for being small, but that didn't change the fact that I was still small. And when I finally got a coon dog pup of my own, I wanted one that was right in every way. It would be the first thing I'd ever owned that didn't have any defects, and I would work myself to death training it to make it not only the best dog it could be, but the best dog in the country. I wanted a dog I could name Chief and have the name fit perfectly, not a dog we already were calling Runt. For all I knew, he wouldn't even open up on a trail.

It was a man from over the other side of Exeter that came and took away the next-to-last pup. It was on a Saturday morning in early October and Daddy was home when he came. As we watched the back of his black buggy growing smaller as he drove away, I felt something tugging at the leg of my overalls. I looked down. It was Runt.

"Look a-here, Daddy. This feller wants to fight," I said, sitting down and rolling the pup around on the new-fallen leaves as he chewed on my fingers.

Daddy chuckled, then stood looking down at me and the pup. Then he spoke.

"Kit, why don't you think about keeping that dog?"

"Huh? Keep him for what?"

"Oh, just for fun. See how he turns out."

I was confused. "But you can sell him. Look at all the money you made on them other pups. He's little, but somebody'll want him. Looks like people around here don't have no better sense." All this time I was still wallowing the pup around while he growled his baby growls and clawed at me.

"Oh, I don't care that much about selling him, Kit. Why don't you keep him and see if he'll make a coon hound? If he does, he can be your dog."

All of a sudden I felt like the sun had gone behind a cloud. I stood up and leaned back against the pickets of the dog fence. I tried to look my father in the eye, but he was too tall and I felt too strange.

"I don't want him for my dog, Daddy. For years I've dreamed of having one and you didn't want another one, so all I could do was go on dreaming. If I ever get to have a dog of my own, I want one that's good stuff to start with so he'll be just right when I get him broke. If we keep this runt, we don't even know if he'll chase a coon or if he'll bark trail. He might be no good at all, and there we'd be with another dog to feed and you'd never let me get the dog I want." I hate to say how close I was to crying, old as I was.

My father was quiet for a moment. I still didn't dare look up for fear he'd see tears on my face. I was looking down at the runt puppy, still tugging at my britches leg. He was cute; all puppies are. But he wasn't right, and he'd never be right. He wasn't made out of the right stuff. Just once in my life, I wanted to have something of my own that was the right stuff.

"Well, all right, son. If you really don't want him, we'll go on and sell him to the next person that comes. I know there's lots of people still wanting one of these pups. Somebody will settle for the runt, especially if we lower the price." And he walked away.

I was almost dizzy, I was so relieved. Daddy had just as good as said he'd let me have one more dog on the place, and once this runt was gone I could start dreaming of my perfect dog again. I sat down on the grass again and went back to playing with the pup.

But the next person didn't come. Days went by and then weeks. We kept hearing from everybody who had bought a pup how they were already, at nine and ten and then twelve weeks, showing signs of brains and hunting savvy like no dog ever seen before. But no one came to get the runt.

It didn't make sense. Most people didn't feel as I did, that they had to have the perfect pup. I would have thought that somebody would offer Daddy a few dollars for the runt and take him home. When he was old enough they'd turn him loose to run with their grown coon dogs and he would start to pick it up. Probably, he'd bark when he was supposed to, but even if he didn't he would earn his keep helping the other dogs track and kill coons. One of the others could do the hollering.

But nobody came. Runt was growing so fast you could almost see it each day. He would never be quite a full sized dog, but he couldn't stay a baby. I got more and more concerned that he was still around. People want to get their dogs as baby pups, so they can break them in as they want to. Older pups have sometimes learned to chase rabbits or have other bad ways, so they can be hard to get rid of. Runt needed to go, and he needed to go soon.

But you know how your heartstrings can get wrapped around a dog.

Chapter 7

A HOME FOR RUNT

If you'd told me when Runt was six weeks old that I'd end up keeping him and loving him like a best friend, I wouldn't have believed it. As I said before, I had dreamed for years of a dog that would be my very own and had the makings of a champion coon dog to start with. What I didn't need was a pup that would never be as big as the others, might not care anything about coons, and might be a silent trailer. That last part wouldn't seem so bad to me now, because if a silent trailer is an extra good dog, you can always hang a bell on his collar or hunt him with another dog that will bark and let you know where they are. But at that time I had my heart set on being independent. I wanted to be able to hunt when I felt like it, depending on myself and my dog, not needing to borrow one of Daddy's dogs to help us. That might not seem important to grown up people, but I was that way and I'll bet I'm not the only boy who ever was, either.

But all that changed one day when Runt was about three months old. That's when a whole lot of other things started changing, too, although I didn't know it then. The turning point was when I got whipped for the third time by Eddie Sloan.

It was November and Simmer and I were starting to do some trapping along Flat Creek. This particular day I was going to meet him after school with a tow sack full of traps and we were going to make some sets farther downstream than we had gone before. I felt sorry for Simmer, because he had to go to school. My mother taught me my lessons right at home, because she had been to eight years of school herself and read a whole lot of books, besides. She said she didn't see any sense in sending me on a three-mile walk every day to get learning she could give me just as easy. That suited me just fine. Simmer had told me about school and I wasn't having any, thank you. He said you had to sit still and not say anything for most of the day. I didn't believe I could have stood it.

He attended Cedar Bluff School, which is across the road from the creek and downstream from the Downs' place. I thought I'd walk to school just as the kids were getting out for the day and walk back home with Simmer so he could change out of his school clothes and we could get about trapping. I'd leave the traps somewhere between his house and the school and we'd hit the creek along in there somewhere.

I left our place with time to spare and picked up my traps from where I had them stashed in the woods near the creek. I had found a hollow stump that just suited for storing traps. I didn't like keeping them at the house when they weren't set, for fear they'd pick up the smell of people or dogs. I wanted them to smell just like the woods so the varmints wouldn't be afraid of them. Besides, steel traps are heavy if you're carrying more than a few of them, and it helps to store them as close as you can to where you're going to set them.

A little while later I passed the road up to Simmer's house and I had no idea that he was already home, having stayed out of school that day because he was sick. Right on past I went, loaded down with my sack of traps so that I was sweating a little even though it was a few days into November. When I thought I was about halfway from Simmer's to the school, I left the road and went a few yards into the woods to hide my traps where nobody would see the sack and wonder what was in it. I'd gone to too much trouble to protect those traps from people smell to have some fool pawing over them. I lined up three big rocks beside the road to show me where to turn off when we came back for them.

I was within a hundred yards of the turnoff to the school when I heard a ruckus around the bend of the road. It sounded like a fight. I broke into a run and hadn't but just reached top speed when I came upon a group of excited little school kids ringed around two older boys who were scrapping in the middle of the road.

If you could call it a scrap. I could see with one eye that it wasn't anything like a fair fight, and when I saw who the boy on top was, I wasn't surprised. It was Eddie Sloan, and, as usual, he was beating up a smaller boy.

He had the other boy down and was sitting astraddle of him, beating him in the face. I couldn't even tell who the other boy was, his nose was bleeding so much and he was so dirty and red in the face from fighting. One of his arms was pinned under Eddie, so he only had one hand to fend off Eddie's punches. He had already taken a bad beating, and Eddie gave no sign of letting up. I knew enough to know Eddie didn't mind hurting someone.

I figured out who the boy on the ground was when I saw little Ora Pyne screaming and crying on the far side of the fight. Ora was about seven or eight years old. She had long braids and a gap where her top front teeth should have been. She kept yelling, "Get off him! You let him up, Eddie Sloan!" and jumping around and crying so I knew it was her brother, Charles, who was getting whipped. I knew Charles well enough to know he hadn't started this fight, and wouldn't have even if he had been Eddie's size. Charles never bothered anybody.

But just then Charles scored a point. Best I could tell, he couldn't really throw a punch, pinned down like he was. But in his thrashing he must have poked Eddie in the eye. Because all of a sudden Eddie jerked upright, cussed and grabbed a rock the size of your fist up out of the road. "I'll knock your brains out!" he screamed.

It takes some time to tell all this, but I had only been standing there about five seconds when Eddie went for the rock. I knew I had to do something then, because the way he raised it up over his head you could tell he meant to kill Charlie with it.

I jumped on Eddie from the side, hitting him as hard as my puny weight would allow. I knew he was mad and wouldn't hold back. And I didn't expect any help from Charlie because he was hurt and winded. So I pounded Eddie with a ferocity that came not from strength but from fear. My first blow caught him squarely on the right ear, and it seemed to stun him. Terrified of the strength he had, I followed with punches as fast and hard as I could deliver them, my fists beating a wap-wap-wap on his head.

I had hunted with hounds a long time, and I knew that when an animal is cornered is when he's the most dangerous. He sees no way out of his trouble but through or over the men or dogs who are threatening him. That's the way it was with me now. I had seen what Eddie had been about to do to Charles Pyne and I had no doubt he would do the same to me if he could.

Bud Carson has lots of favorite sayings. One of them is, "It ain't the size of the dog in the fight, it's the size of the fight in the dog." I think Eddie Sloan was a little surprised at the size of the fight in me that day. First was the shock of being jumped on by somebody he didn't even know was there, then there was the fact that I was fresh while he had already fought one fight, and all that was on top of the fact that I was scared half to death. I believe I hit harder and faster than I ever had in my life.

So when Eddie finally scrambled out from under me and got to his feet, he didn't look as mad as I would have expected. He looked some mad, but a little bit shaken, too. I didn't dare back off to see if he'd quit; I knew he wouldn't. I just kept taking the fight to him, trying to keep him so busy warding off my punches that he couldn't concentrate enough to get all his strength behind one of those big-knuckled fists of his. It almost looked like I could give him a fair match. Finally, though, I lost my balance and fell into him. He grabbed for my head and next thing I knew, he had me in a headlock. I thought it was all over then, for sure. But he had his right arm around my head, so that he had to hit me with his left, which wasn't as potent. Thanks to that and the fact that my face was more pinned against his side than exposed to his punches, I took most of the beating on the top of my head, which Daddy always said was hard enough to shatter hailstones. I wasn't hurt too badly to think what to do, and when I thought of it I did it. I sank my teeth into his side like a hungry dog would grab a pork chop.

The howl Eddie let out then made his screaming and cussing at Charles sound like a whisper. His arm had felt like a band of iron around my head, but suddenly it was gone as he let go his hold and jumped away from me. That is, he tried to jump away from me, but I didn't let go. I was afraid to. So I wrapped my arms around him and clamped my teeth together with all the strength in my jaws, staggering after him as he leaped and danced around on the gravel of the road. I don't know how long that went on. I felt half crazy as he dragged me around after him, screaming and cussing and pounding on me as much as our awkward position would allow. The little kids scattered from us like chickens, running in all directions to get out of the way. I was jerked off my feet and felt the rocks and gravel of the road dig into my bare feet and ankles. Still I hung on like a snapping turtle, afraid of what would happen if I let go.

Suddenly I heard a yell that didn't come from Eddie. It was a man's voice yelling, "Stop it! Stop it, you two!" and I felt a hand grab my shirt collar, not gently. I relaxed my bite just half a second and that was enough. The hand jerked me away from Eddie and sent me spinning across the road, barely keeping my feet under me. I was still scared and excited, and as soon as my eyes started to focus I grabbed up two big rocks out of the road and turned to face Eddie in case he came after me.

But he wasn't going anywhere. Mr. Bruce, the school teacher, had grabbed Eddie by the collar as soon as he had let go of mine. He was a great big man, about fifty years old and looked about as much like a school teacher as I did a tomcat. If you'd told me he was half grizzly bear I'd have believed it.

"All right, what's going on here?" he demanded of nobody in particular, although I noticed he looked more at Eddie than anybody else. He must have heard a yell from the group around the fight as he left the school going home the other way on the road.

There was a second or two of quiet when all you could hear was the sobbing breaths Eddie and I were struggling to pull into our lungs. Then Ora Pyne spoke up.

"Eddie jumped on Charles, Mr. Bruce! For no reason at all. He had Charles down and was just about to hit him in the head with a rock when Kit came along and jumped on him. He would have killed Charles, Mr. Bruce!"

All the other little kids said the same thing. Eddie looked awful sheepish with Mr. Bruce's big paw holding him so easily by the scruff of the neck. Like most bullies, he got real meek when there was somebody around who was bigger and stronger than he was. Mr. Bruce was very red in the face, as if he would have liked nothing better than to pick up Eddie and break him in half.

"Edward Sloan, you are in very deep trouble," Mr. Bruce said without moving his jaws. "I will be at your home tomorrow to have a talk with your parents. And if that doesn't take care of your behavior, we'll see what the law has to say about assault and battery. Do you understand me?" He had Eddie up on tiptoes and was talking to him from about six inches away.

"Y-y-yessir!" Eddie quavered. He looked like a scared three-year-old.

"Now get out of my sight!" Mr. Bruce roared, giving Eddie a sling that sent him skittering across the gravel for ten feet.

Eddie didn't waste time. He headed down the road at a gallop. Mr. Bruce turned to Charles.

"Charles, are you all right?" All of a sudden there was gentleness in his voice. He had turned from a bear to a lamb.

"Yes, sir, I think so," Charles answered. He was holding a dead tree limb in his hand and it came to me in a rush that he had just gotten up off the ground and found a club to help me with Eddie. It made me feel good inside that he would do that after already having taken a beating. He had a black eye, a couple of bruises on his face and his nose was still bleeding a little. His lower lip was cut and swelling.

Mr. Bruce looked him over a minute, frowning. "Yes, I believe you'll live." He pulled out a handkerchief and brushed some of the dirt off Charles' face and dabbed at the bleeding. "Here, hold this against your nose until you can get home and get cleaned up."

He turned to me. "Kit, are you hurt?" He put his hand on my shoulder to look at me and again I felt the gentleness that filled this great big man.

"I believe I'm all right, sir. I'm glad you came when you did, though." And I never spoke a truer word in my life.

Then I asked him if Simmer was around and he said no, that word had come that Simmer was sick. If I'd known that, I could have saved myself some bruises. For Charles' sake, though, I reckon it was good I came along when I did.

Mr. Bruce looked around the scattered circle of big-eyed children. "Is anyone else hurt?" he asked.

71

They all said, "No, Mr. Bruce. No sir, Mr. Bruce. No, sir."

"All right then, you'd better all go on home. And I promise you, there will be no more trouble for any of you out of Eddie Sloan."

The group scattered as the kids moved off by ones and twos, carrying their books by straps over their shoulders and talking in low tones, as if they were still scared.

Charles came over to me and stuck out his hand. I shook it. Handshaking was a little more formal than what I was used to among the boys, but it seemed right because of what had just happened.

"Thanks, Kit," Charles said. "I reckon Eddie would've brained me if you hadn't jumped in when you did."

"Aw, you'd have done the same for me. Fact is, it looked like you were going to, 'til Mr. Bruce showed up."

Charles chuckled through his swollen lips. "Yep. If Mr. Bruce hadn't been there, you and me and this here hickory limb would have broke old Eddie from sucking eggs."

That was a cheerful thought, and I chewed it over as I walked home. I was hopeful maybe Mr. Bruce had put a fear of judgment in Eddie Sloan. There are too many Eddies in the world, always looking for somebody smaller and weaker to pick on just for fun. They should all run into a Mr. Bruce.

It occurred to me as I walked along that helping Charles had been the right thing to do. I didn't have to do it, but it seemed right and it was. Now that I thought of it, it was my way to side with the underdog. I knew what it felt like to be smaller and weaker than the other boys, and it wasn't fun. There are always people like Eddie who laugh at you or pick on you for things that aren't any of your fault. The more I thought about it, the more wrong it seemed for the strong to trouble the weak.

The thought stayed with me all the way home. Sometimes I had felt that I was all alone in the world in a way. That is, that I was a runt and nobody else really knew how it felt but me. But there was Charles. He wasn't really a runt, but he was younger and smaller than Eddie. I was glad I had mixed in his fight. Mama says God doesn't like fighting, and I know she's right. But I hadn't fought for fun or to hurt somebody or because I was mad. I had fought to help somebody who needed help and hadn't done anything wrong.

Yes, that suited me just right. Some of this world's creatures start out on top, with everything going their way. But others have lots of things against them from the beginning, and I knew how they felt. I made up my mind that I would always take the side of the underdog. He was the one who needed help, who needed a friend, and a friend of the underdog is what I would be.

I was thinking hard on that thought, looking down at the gravel as I walked along the road. I didn't even realize I was almost home until I heard Bruisin' Susan and the other dogs baying at me from their pen. The first thing I saw when I looked up was Runt.

Chapter 8

TRAINING THE PUP

That's when it hit me. Runt was an underdog.

He was too little, just like me. And he had it even worse than I did. His blood was all mixed up. Nobody knew if he was a bloodhound or a coonhound and so nobody wanted anything to do with him. Oh, they'd all been eager to take a chance on the other pups. They were big and healthy-looking. In fact, they were even bigger than average coon hound pups because of their father's size. That didn't mean they'd be any good as hunters, but it made for a good appearance. But not Runt.

The other pups had looked like coon dogs, mostly black with some tan markings, like Bruisin' Susan. Runt looked like neither Susan nor Buck. He wasn't black with some tan, like his mother, or tan all over, like his father. He was mostly tan, but he had a black saddle and some other black markings. He was heavier-boned, more like a bloodhound, which meant he wouldn't be a fast runner. Because he would never be as tall as a normal hound, he would have more trouble getting through high weeds and such. About all that was left was nose and courage, and there was no way to tell yet about either one.

Runt met me while I was still in the road. He stood up on his hind legs, pawing at me and whining with eagerness to play. I stopped and bent over to pat him, getting a sloppy lick across the nose for my trouble. When I straightened up and started toward the house, he grabbed onto the leg of my overalls and went to growling and tugging. I dragged him into the yard, then sat down in the grass and went to rough-housing with him.

Puppies love to play. Runt let go of my overalls when I sat down and jumped up in my face, knocking me over backward in the grass. Then he pounced on my chest and tried again to slap my face clear off my head with his sloppy tongue. I rolled away from him and kept on rolling, while he came pouncing and yapping after me. I stopped on my stomach and hid my face in my arms, but he wasn't discouraged. He kept climbing over my shoulders and scrambling in half-circles around my head, trying to find a hole in my defenses to lick me through. He tried to bite me on the back of the head, then tried to dig me out, leaving several white scratches on my arms and neck where he clawed me. That persuaded me to turn over, so I rolled to my back and sat up where I could defend myself better.

Then he wanted to run. He took off running straight away from me as fast as his stubby little legs would carry him. He turned to see if I was chasing him, and promptly tripped over his own big feet, sprawling tip-over-teakettle with a grunt. Then he came running back as if to run right over me. I got on all fours like I was another dog wanting to fight, crouching and snarling as he approached. At the last second I made a grab at him, but he was faster than he looked and leaped aside. I sprawled on my face. That was his opening to jump in and bite me on the right ear. I yowled as his needle-sharp baby teeth sank much too deep for play, and turned to a sitting position again, holding my ear. Runt ran another half-circle then bored in again, his long ears flapping with each jump and his tail held out sideways in a foolish-looking half-curl. This time I was ready for him and timed my grab perfectly. He yelped as if he'd been stung when I grabbed him.

"Hah! Got you, you little devil!" I yelled in triumph. I wrestled him a little more, his back to the ground and all four feet clawing at me while his sharp puppy teeth clamped on my jacket sleeve. What a savage. I stood up and headed toward the house with Runt yapping and snarling behind me, trying for another grip on my britches leg.

I managed to shake him loose coming up the porch steps and shut the screen door behind me before he could slip through. Runt scratched at the screen and yipped indignantly. Then he gave it up and lay down in his usual spot, right against the screen door so nobody could open it.

I stood in the doorway for a couple of minutes, looking out through the screen at my little valley. It occurred to me that the Ozarks were a great place to live. Our house was at the end of a long section of bottom land, embraced by ridges on the sides and divided unevenly down the middle by Flat Creek where it rippled through its twisting, rocky bed. Looking upstream you could see a mile or more on a clear day, and it was worth the looking. Even now, in early November, there was a lot of October color left on the trees. The grass in the pasture by the creek was still plenty green, as well. Right here at suppertime was a good time to be looking. The sun was following its autumn custom of going to bed early, making the tops of the ridges seem to catch fire as the colorful leaves glowed with the first rays of sundown.

It was a peaceful time. The lines of the landscape were softened by the waning light as the shadows began to creep across the pastures and woods. The light breeze of the afternoon had died and the air was now still as a cemetery, so calm you could hear the creek rushing over the rocks under the little wooden bridge down the road toward Star City.

Suddenly I began to feel thankful. I'd had a rough afternoon, but everything really was all right. I was home, home at our white frame house on the Flat Creek road. I had my mama who loved me and Daddy, the honest and respected sheriff of Barry County. We had our little farm and our creek and our friends. We had our woods and our hills.

Our land was rocky, and that made it a little hard to work. Our neighbor, Mr. Ash, went out to Kansas once and he says there are places out there where you could plow all day and never hit a rock. But it's dry, and the land is flat and sandy. The soil sprouts sandburrs that stick to your shoestrings in clumps and fill the dogs' feet with their stinging spines. Give me my rocky hills. Oh, sure, the ticks and chiggers are an irritation in the warm months. But you can sprinkle your clothes with sulfur and they won't bother you. I'd rather have chiggers year 'round than have to put up with city noise or the constant, drying wind of the plains. No, my little valley was just right for me.

And I had my dog. Now I knew why nobody had taken Runt; he was being saved for me. He and I belonged together because we were both runts and underdogs. We could understand each other.

And I was determined to make him a winner. Looking at him now, flopped on the sawmill boards of the porch floor, I felt a little like I had when I saw Charles Pyne getting beaten up by Eddie Sloan. This little dog hadn't done anything wrong, yet he was getting a bad deal. He was unwanted. Well, I wanted him now. I was going to be on his side and I intended to make him the best hound dog that ever treed a coon. As soon as Daddy got home from town, I'd tell him I'd changed my mind.

And that was the beginning of a new chapter in my life. From that day on, Runt followed me almost everywhere I went. We'd been keeping him pretty much confined when I wasn't home so he wouldn't get out of pocket and maybe end up in trouble. We hadn't been doing anything with him, because we hadn't planned to keep him. But now I started letting him follow me around while I did my chores, ran my trap line, went fishing with Simmer or just rambled.

It was fall and we had taken the three grown dogs on a couple of hunts already. But Runt was too small to even begin to keep up on a chase, so I couldn't train him in the usual way—that is, just let him run with the big dogs until instinct took over and he picked it up. I couldn't stand the thought of waiting until the following season, either, so I asked my father and the other coon hunters I knew, what I could do to start training Runt. They gave me some ideas, and Runt and I were off and running.

I enlisted Simmer to help me. The first time we caught a coon in one of our traps, we skinned it and fed part of the meat to Runt. He acted like it tasted a little strange and wouldn't eat much. But he loved the skin. We teased him with it, yelling and acting all excited like it was a wonderful new toy. He looked plenty foolish, jumping up in the air trying to grab the flapping tail as we whipped and dangled it just beyond his reach. Once in a while we'd let him get ahold of it and he'd tug on it and shake it back and forth just like killing a rat, growling savagely the whole time. It was exciting when he did that. It made me think maybe the coon scent was triggering something deep inside him, telling him that even though he was just a baby, this smell was the thing he he had been born to hunt. Mama warned me not to be too confident though, because the little scoundrel would do the same thing to anything on the clothesline that hung low enough for him to reach it.

Simmer suggested leaving Runt penned up more.

"Maybe if you brought out the coonskin and shook it at him every time you let him out, it'd make him more excited to see it. He might get the idea that the reason he gets out of the pen is to tackle a coon."

We tried it and, sure enough, it seemed to have an effect. I not only teased him with the skin whenever I let him out, but whenever I fed him, too. He got fed twice a day because he was young and it gave me a lot of chances to play with him with the skin. As the weeks went by, Runt got to where he'd start yelping and pawing at the gate whenever I took the skin out from the woodshed where I kept it and waved it around.

After a month of this play, Simmer and I had to sacrifice four bits and reserve another coon skin. The first one had lost a lot of its hair in its battles with Runt and we thought it might be losing its scent, too. So the next coonskin we harvested from the trapline went into the woodshed instead of being stretched on a board. I burned the old one to make sure Runt wouldn't ever get hold of it and maybe chew it up and choke on a piece of it. You can't be too careful with puppies; they do some silly things.

I enjoyed my training sessions with Runt a lot more when Simmer was along, but we were limited by the fact that he had to waste an awful lot of time in school. By the time he got out for the day, there was only a little daylight left. So we were tickled when December came and we heard that school was going to close for two whole weeks around Christmas and New Year's. We could get in a lot of hunting and trapping and have lots of time for Runt, too.

The first day of Christmas vacation, Simmer was at my house by daybreak to check the trapline. This was something I had been doing by myself except on weekends, because he didn't have time between his morning farm chores and school. It was cold that day, but the sky was bright clear blue above the brown winter landscape. It took us an hour and a half to work our way along the creek, checking our sets and skinning our varmints. As we went, we talked over different ideas for training Runt.

Runt had been doing well. He loved to see me bring the coonskin out of the woodshed, knowing when he saw it that he was going to be let out of his pen to play or that it was mealtime. He would get so excited that he'd turn circles around himself until he'd fall down if I didn't open the pen gate fast enough to suit him. The yelping and bawling was some kind of racket. There was no question whether he had the interest to chase a coon. The next thing was to teach him to look for coons, rather than waiting for somebody to flap the tail of a skin in his face.

"I've got an idea," Simmer said as we fought our way through waist-high bushes toward the brushpile where our last two traps were set. "Let's try hiding the skin from him. We've got him where he wants it bad enough. How 'bout if you hold him while I take the skin and tease him with it and then run into the barn or into a patch of thick brush like this and hide the skin. Then you turn him loose and he goes in to find it."

I thought a second as I kicked loose from a wild grape vine that had wrapped itself around my left ankle. "That makes sense," I told him. "We can get to playing tug-of-war with him, then when he's good and wound up, yank the skin away and run off with it."

When we got back to the house we stretched our few pelts on boards and threw them up on the chicken house roof to dry. Then we went to get Runt and his coonskin.

"You goin' to give him his mornin' feedin' first?" Simmer asked.

"I thought maybe I wouldn't. You reckon he'd be more eager to hunt if I didn't? Bud always says the hungry dog runs fastest."

"Maybe so. I know I don't feel like moving real fast right after a big supper." I could have said that Simmer didn't seem to feel like moving real fast very often anyway, but he probably wouldn't have known what I was talking about.

We got the coonskin down from where we kept it hung on a nail high in the woodshed. Runt had heard us talking as we were coming from the chicken house and he had already joined the older dogs in giving us a loud good morning. I mean to tell you, four hounds can make a racket that will make you deaf or make you wish you were. When we appeared around the corner of the woodshed by Runt's pen with his play skin, he came unglued as usual.

He started jumping around the pen, bouncing off the gate, turning circles and yelping in his little high-pitched puppy yowl while his long ears flapped against his head. Then Simmer got into the act, and I mean I never saw the like.

Simmer was carrying the skin. As soon as Runt went into his routine, Simmer started acting like he'd lost his marbles. He flapped the skin, which sort of rattled because it was stiff as a board. The noise always excited Runt, and the whipping of the furry tail riled him even more. Simmer made it even better than usual, running back and forth along the fence, yelling like an Indian, beating the fence with the skin, jumping and waving his arms. I never saw Runt carry on like he did then. Maybe he was surprised, as I was, that Simmer Downs had that much life in him.

"Let him out, Kit!" Simmer yelled above the frenzied yelping and baying of the dogs, and took off running across the yard. I opened the gate, and Runt never had a word for me. He took out across the grass after Simmer and that skin like he was going to tear them both to pieces. Simmer was acting like he was fighting that coon, and maybe getting the worst of it. He waved it over his head and all around him as he ran, yelping and screaming as if it had all of its teeth and claws sunk in and ripping him. Runt caught up in just a few jumps.

Simmer stopped running then, and just danced around, whooping and hollering and waving the skin. It was some kind of a sight. Simmer acting as if he had a nest of yellow jackets inside his overalls and lttle Runt howling and jumping up on him, trying to get in on the fight and getting madder and madder as Simmer kept yanking the skin away just as Runt's teeth were about to snap shut on it. Finally,

Simmer let him get a hold on the skin and dropped to his knees to play tug-of-war.

Runt loved this game, and today he was really primed. I had to admit Simmer was sure handling him well, jerking and shaking the skin enough to keep Runt excited, but not quite hard enough to pull it away. And all the time, he kept up his yelling and carrying on. Then all of a sudden, he yelled, "Catch him, Kit!" and as soon as I did he pulled the skin away and ran into the barn.

Runt was really fit to be tied then. He had just lit into that coon and it had escaped. It was all I could do to hold him as he scrambled and fought me. And what made it even harder was that I was laughing until the tears came at him being so crazy to get at a coon that was already dead and the way Simmer was acting like a lunatic. He whined and yelped, jumping toward the barn where he could hear Simmer rustling around in the hay as he hid the skin. Then I heard Simmer yell again.

"Let him go, Kit!" So I let him go and he tore out of my arms so fast that he got his big feet tangled up and sprawled forward on his chest, nearly knocking the wind out of himself. But not quite. He got right side up in a flash and away he went, racing out of the yard, across the barnyard and into the big double front doors where he had seen Simmer disappear. I was close behind him, making none-too-good time because of trying to run and laugh and cry all at the same time.

When I got inside the barn I couldn't see just right because my eyes were used to the bright December sunlight outside and the barn was a little gloomy. But I could hear Runt tearing through the hay, looking for that coonskin.

Simmer had stopped acting like a drunk Indian and was following Runt around the barn yelling encouragement.

"Atta boy, Runt! Get him, boy! Tear that coon up!" I joined in for a minute, then asked him where he had hidden the skin.

"It's in the feed rack," he said.

We had racks in the barn that were made slatted, with the boards a few inches apart so the stock could pull hay out to eat it without dragging huge clumps out to get trampled under foot and wasted. The bottom of a rack was a couple of feet off the floor, so the skin must be hidden in the hay, well higher than Runt's head. It was interesting to stand and watch him searching for it, yelling and clapping our hands to encourage him and keep him excited. I'd seen the effects of the pack instinct before. You put four dogs in a pen and as soon as one sees something to bark at, the rest all get steamed up and go to hollering, too. I had no way of knowing, but I had the feeling that I could work the same way with Runt. Which wouldn't matter when he was older and chasing real coons miles out in the woods, but it might help a lot in his puppy training.

Runt was taking his job seriously. He wasn't wasting time looking around as if he hoped to see the coon climbing one of the cedar posts that held up the hayloft, but going straight to his nose for help. He was moving around the barn at a fast trot, whining and snuffling and every now and then standing up on his hind legs with a forefoot against the wall to smell the air above his head. He trotted right past the hay rack, then suddenly whipped around and went back the other direction. He almost passed the rack again, but then his little head went up and he stood up on his back legs, pawing at the bottom of the rack and yelping and whining with everything he had. Then he was jumping up and down, trying to find a way into that rack to dig his arch enemy out of the hay.

We let him fuss for a minute, then Simmer stepped past him and reached deep into the loose hay of the rack. He pulled the skin out and Runt didn't even give him time to shake the hay off before starting to climb Simmer's overalls to get at that varmint. Simmer lowered it to where Runt could just jump and get it, then as soon as he had latched onto it started playing tug-of-war with him again, yelling encouragement all the time. It was hard to decide which of them looked sillier.

Finally, I grabbed Runt and pulled him away. He fought me and yowled, but this time I was ready and managed to hang on. "Stay here a minute," I said to Simmer. I want to pen him up 'fore we do any more."

Simmer left the coonskin around the corner of the woodshed when he came back to the pen.

"Well, what d'you think of that?" he asked, still panting. He looked plenty pleased with both Runt and us.

I shook my head. "Simmer, you really had him going. He was as shook up 'bout that old skin as I've ever seen him. And didn't he do a job of finding it in the hay?"

We stood leaning on the fence and looking at the long-eared little pup who was still whining and clawing at the wire, stopping every few seconds to point his black nose up in the air and give a baby howl. He hadn't been nearly ready to quit, which is just what I wanted. Simmer's grandad, who had trained a lot of good stock dogs, had warned us to stop our training sessions before the dog had time to get tired of it. He said you should always leave a dog wanting more, and that young pups especially had short attention spans. So we fed Runt and left him for a while. Simmer helped me with some chores I had to do, and that took up the rest of the morning. Mama fed us beef stew for dinner, and in between bites of stew and cornbread we talked.

We talked about what we'd do next with Runt and how he was going to be the world's best coon dog in a few months and how we'd divide the money we got for the pelts he got us. Simmer didn't think he had anything coming since Runt was my dog, but I said no, he was doing just as much of the training as I was and he would get a share. Over apple pie and milk we discussed what all we'd spend our money on and how long it would be before we had new repeating rifles and saddle horses like Bud's. We agreed it wouldn't take long.

After dinner we went back to work on Runt. He met us at the gate of his pen again, whining and wagging his whole caboose as if his tail alone just wouldn't do the job. We didn't go straight for the coonskin, but let him out to run a little bit while we talked about what to work him on next.

Simmer said, "Looks to me like he's ready to start tracking. He's proved he'll chase the coonskin. Even when he can't see it."

"Yeah, he's started using his nose," I answered. "What d'you reckon the next step ought to be?"

"Why don't we try dragging the skin on the ground and see if he'll run the track?"

"You reckon he would?"

"I'll bet so."

I thought about it a minute. "All right, tell you what. Let's tie a piece of rope on the skin and drag it around the yard and let him chase it. Then, when he's got the idea of chasing the thing across the ground, you can take off around the corner of the house into the field dragging the skin, and I'll hold Runt where he can't see which way you went. Then he'll have to go to his nose. You go a ways out into the field and lay down in the grass where he can't see you and I'll turn him loose to track you down. When he gets to you, jump up and flap the skin at him and play tug-of-war with him until I catch him and call him off. We'll make it a new game. Like hide-and-seek."

So that's what we did. We found a piece of thin rope that Daddy had used for plow lines until he got his good leather ones and cut two pieces off it. We tied one piece to the coonskin to make it easier to drag and the other around Runt's neck. I didn't have a collar small enough for him, so this would have to do for now. It was better than having to wrestle him all the time.

I held tight to Runt's rope while Simmer ran around the corner of the house, dragging the skin and whooping like a crazy man. I don't think Runt really needed the yelling to excite him, what with that skin scraping and bouncing over the grass. He fought the rope, plunging and rearing and shaking his head like a bass fighting the hook. He wanted to chase that skin something awful. When I heard Simmer holler that he was ready I dropped the rope and let Runt take off. He was gone like a bullet, rounding the corner of the house so fast his feet almost slid out from under him. I was a second behind him, and expected to find him flying along Simmer's track out into the field. But he had stopped dead in his tracks.

He was used to being able to see the skin and now he didn't see the skin or Simmer, either one. He stood and sniffed the air a second or two, then took off sprinting around the next corner of the house. Again he stopped, standing there whining and looking foolish. I ran up behind him and grabbed the dragging end of the rope.

"Back around here, dummy," I told him. I pulled on the rope gently and started back to the side yard, coaxing him to follow me. I could see where Simmer had left the yard and started across the pasture by the bent-over grass. It seemed that Runt had run right off the track, I guess because he had thought he'd be able to see the skin like before. I thought I might have to help him a little, since there was bound to be coon scent all over the yard where we had been playing with it. But first I wanted to try walking him across the track and see if he'd think to use his nose if I made him go slow enough.

I pulled him out to the edge of the yard and walked along it. He fought the rope some, not being used to it. But he didn't seem to think about it much. Mostly he was looking for that skin. And sure enough, after he'd tried a minute to get away from me so he could run around looking, he seemed to give it up and start depending on his nose.

A little of the scent must have drifted through the air toward us, because Runt suddenly seemed to get a new burst of excitement. He allowed me to lead him along the barbed wire fence of the pasture and I could see we were heading straight for the place where Simmer had scooted under. Then we came to the very spot and Runt shoved his little nose into the trampled brown grass. Whining, grunting and snuffling, he slid under the bottom wire.

He was tracking! There was no question now. He hit the end of his fifteen-foot rope before I could get across the fence and almost pulled my arm out of socket. Then he

88

plunged and bucked and fought, growling and trying to back out of the loop around his neck.

"All right, all right. Keep your britches on," I told him. "I'm coming fast as I can." I had tried to squeeze between the wires of the fence, thinking it would be a little quicker than crawling under. But I was wrong. With Runt tugging on the rope as hard as he could, and me laughing so hard at the fuss he was making, I couldn't seem to get unhooked from all the places my clothes were caught on the wire. Finally I did get through, and we took off across the field. It wasn't easy running for the pup. His short legs had trouble in the tall, dead grass. But he made good enough headway that it was all I could do to keep up. His nose was up, because the skin had scraped over the grass, not right down on the ground. But still I could tell he was trailing by scent. There was nothing for Runt to see, but he was pulling confidently on the rope. He knew exactly where that skin had gone.

We had only gone about fifty yards when Simmer jumped up and took off. When Simmer had taken just a few steps, the slack came out of his rope and yanked that coonskin up out of the grass where he had hidden it, just a second before Runt pounced at it. Runt went crazy. He yelped and flung himself after Simmer so hard that it yanked the rope out of my hand. In a few jumps he had caught up with the skin and was working it over.

Simmer turned around for a tugging contest. He gave Runt a good tussle, then turned loose of the skin and let Runt have it. Runt growled and shook the skin ferociously for a moment, then seemed to realize that the skin had stopped fighting. He dropped to his belly then rolled on his back, chewing the edge of the stiff hide for all his puppy teeth were worth.

"Look at that! He thinks he killed it!" Simmer was laughing fit to bust, and so was I. Runt just looked so funny, acting as if he'd whipped a coon and was starting to eat it. He was biggest dog on the porch now.

We were new in the dog training business, but Simmer and I felt that we were over a hump then. Runt had gone from playing with the skin, which any puppy would have done, to finding it by scent in the barn, to tracking it across the ground. It looked like now it was just a matter of making the tracks longer and more difficult until he was big and fast enough to chase real coons with the grown dogs.

Every day for the rest of Simmer's Christmas recess, we worked Runt on his tracking. One of us would hold Runt back while the other started a track out of his sight, then turn him loose and follow. We changed coonskins again, hoping the fresher scent would help keep Runt interested. We made the tracks longer each day, adding little twists and turns to keep Runt alert and make him depend on his nose rather than just starting in one direction and staying with it. We dragged the skin through fields, woods, pastures, barn lots and once, through our house. Only once, because Mama wasn't as excited about the training as we were.

Then school started again, and I was left on my own most of the time. It was harder now, because without somebody to hold Runt I had to tie him up, lay the track, leave the skin hidden, and circle back to let him go run the track. It wasn't as much fun without Simmer, but we stayed after it and Runt kept getting better. Gradually, I left him tied longer before turning him loose to hunt the skin. At first five minutes, then ten, then twenty, and on up to two hours. He was learning to follow a cold trail.

Simmer helped us on Saturdays. One cold afternoon in February we were standing on a frosty hilltop, huddling in our coats and watching while Runt followed the track Simmer had made an hour earlier. I had turned Runt loose and let him get far ahead of me on the trail before turning back and circling around the other side of the hill to climb up and join Simmer at the top. Simmer had used all kinds of tricks to hide the trail, dragging the skin in circles, holding it up off the ground for a few steps and jumping from rock to rock where he could. It was a treat to be able to stand on that hilltop and watch my dog work out each maneuver as he came to it. Then I thought of something.

"Hey, Simmer," I said suddenly.

"Hey, yourself."

"How do we know what he's tracking?"

"Huh?"

"How do we know he's tracking the skin? I mean, he could be tracking you. You've been everywhere the skin has."

He took his eyes off Runt and looked at me. "You know, that's right. When one of us drags that skin, we probably leave more smell than it does. You reckon Runt might get lazy sometimes and just follow our smell when the coon scent's weak?"

"I wouldn't doubt it a bit," I told him.

We both stood there thinking about that. We knew we might not be doing Runt any good if he was getting the idea that all he had to do to find a coon was follow people scent.

The thought struck me that since he was part man dog, it might be extra confusing.

"He'll probably be all right when he gets old enough to keep up with the old dogs, won't he?" proposed Simmer. "I mean, he's got the idea of chasing the coonskin. Surely when he starts going with the pack he'll learn right quick that you don't find coons by follering man scent."

"Well, yes, surely he will. The other dogs'll soon teach him that." Still, I frowned, thinking.

"Then maybe we just shouldn't worry about it. We don't even have to keep on training him. If we want to, we could just wait a couple more months and turn him loose with the big dogs."

Simmer was always just not worrying about something.

"But we're having fun training Runt. I don't want to have to quit just because he might get a little confused about what he's tracking." I stopped. An idea had come to me. "Hey, I'll tell you what, Simmer. Let's tie the skin rope to the end of a long pole so we can hold it out to the side and not mix the coon trail with our own. You could even walk along a fence and drag the skin along the other side if you wanted to."

Simmer said that sounded all right, so we found a sapling the right length and started using it to hold the skin at a distance while dragging it. When I started Runt on the track in the grass, he stayed with it to the end. The pole seemed to be the answer to our problem, but it was awfully unhandy. It was so awkward that it wore us out to drag the skin very far. Finally we slacked off to where we just weren't doing much tracking with Runt at all. It wasn't as much fun having to use that awkward pole, and we thought we had him pretty well started, anyway. He'd be too young to hunt this season, and by next fall when hunting started again he would be ready to hunt with the pack. He really didn't need a lot more help from us.

I was satisfied with the way Runt had come along through the fall and winter. I felt that I'd kept the promise I had made the day I came home from fighting Eddie Sloan. I had kept Runt and worked hard with him. I figured he'd learn what I hadn't been able to teach him, when he started hunting with the other dogs next season, and after that I'd hunt him so much that he'd just naturally become the best coon hound in Barry County. But as Granny James says, the Lord works in mysterious ways. I never would have guessed that Runt's first hunt might come in the summer. Or that his first coon fight might be his last.

Chapter 9

COON FIGHT

If I had to pick my favorite month of the year, I don't know if I'd pick May or June or July. It would be one of the warm months for sure, but not August because that's when you have the hot, humid dog days and when there's most likely to be a drought. I like July because most of the garden is ripening then, and I do love fresh roasting ears and tomatoes. June is awfully nice too, because even though most of the fruits and vegetables aren't ripe, everything on the farm and in the woods is green and humming with life.

June is when the first cutting of hay comes, and I always liked that. Because Daddy stayed busy with his sheriffing, I got to do a lot of the farm work that other boys my age didn't, like ride the horse-drawn mower and dump rake. Another thing about June is that nothing looks tired yet. I don't know if you know what I mean, but in July the locust leaves start turning brown and it sort of reminds you that summer can't last forever and cold weather will come again. In June there's none of that. Everything still looks new.

Still I might just pick May for my favorite. It's not full-grown summer yet, with the leaves all on the trees and the garden plants well up, but it's a time when you feel so many new beginnings. May is when the water in the creek gets warm enough so the bass start biting well and you can swim without your teeth chattering. It's when the garden is mostly planted, so you're done with that, and starting to see lots of new baby plants peeking out of the soil. All danger of frost is past, so you can plant anything you want and don't have to worry about it getting cold-shocked. There are lots of baby animals and birds around. You can take the heating stove down and put it in the woodshed; if there is a chilly day the cookstove will be more than enough. When May comes, all the discomfort of winter is far enough away that you can forget it, like a bruise that's almost healed.

But the best thing of all about May is that that's when school gets out for the summer. I used to yearn for the last day of school almost as much as the school kids did, because when spring came around I just naturally figured boys should be outdoors. And for me that meant outdoors with Simmer Downs.

I was waiting on the road in front of Cedar Bluff school when Mr. Bruce rang the dismissal bell for the last time that term. I didn't have to worry about meeting Eddie Sloan again because his family had moved away the month before. They had said they were selling out because the old farm was just too rocky and rough to make a living. But the story going around was that somebody had finally taken sick and died from drinking Mr. Sloan's corn liquor and so his main business had gone under. Either way, nobody missed them much. Mama said it was too bad that us church people hadn't reached them for the Lord. Mama has a way of saying things that take all the fun out of your spite.

When the door opened and the school kids came flooding out, Mr. Bruce stood on the steps and shook hands with each one of them, little ones first and then the big kids as they filed through the door. When Simmer saw me he grinned and waved. Then it was his turn to shake with Mr. Bruce and I saw the teacher tousle his hair before he turned to the next kid. I guess a teacher as big as Mr. Bruce can afford to be friendly. Simmer hung his book strap over his shoulder and came down the path almost at a trot behind the smaller kids. There must have been twenty-five school kids, more than you'd think would live in the whole county.

"No more school!" Simmer grinned as he punched me on the arm. I punched him back and we started down the road toward his house.

"And ain't I glad," I said. "We've got a whole summer's loafing and fishing to do, and it's high time we got started on it. Did you ask your ma if you could stay at our house tonight?"

"Yep. She said, fine. What's for supper?" Simmer was always interested in supper.

"Pork chops. I told Mama today was the last day of school, so she said bring you home this evening and she'd cook your favorite."

His face took on that lazy, contented smile. "You got a good mama, Kit."

It was one of those good feeling times. Walking home in the spring sunshine with my best friend, then waiting on his front steps while he changed out of his school clothes. His father opened the screen door and stepped out on the porch with me. He was a nice man, Mr. Downs. Always joking with us boys and letting us have a watermelon from the garden when we really needed one. He was about average size, a little thick through the middle and always wearing a trace of a grin as if he knew something funny that he wasn't quite ready to tell yet.

"Well, howdy, Kit. How're you and that fancy coon dog?" Simmer had told him all about training Runt.

"We're fine, Mr. Downs. Haven't done much with Runt for a couple of months, but he's growing up. He looks good."

"Mm-hmm," he said in an encouraging tone. "Is he barking on trail yet?"

I shook my head. "No, sir. Don't know if he'll ever open up, being half bloodhound."

"Well, that ain't no big deal. Long as he kin track and fight, you can always hunt him with another dog to do the barking."

"That's what I figure. But he's only nine months old. He may start opening up yet."

"Well, that's true, that's true. I run into Moe Benner th' other day. He said that pup he got from your pa ran some this winter and opened up just like an old dog. Said he worked good, too. But they don't all start at the same age, you know."

That was true. Some dogs didn't open on trail until they were around a year old. It was just too early to tell. One thing for sure, Runt knew how to track. And he didn't have to have any help from another dog to do it.

Simmer came out then. He looked better in his old overalls and without a strap of books weighing him down. I got up from the steps.

97

"So long, Mr. Downs."

"So long, Kit. Simmer, don't you eat Mr. and Mrs. Hunt out of house and home like you do us, now." He grinned and we grinned back at him as we walked out through the gate and down the road.

Next day we were up before the sun. Simmer helped me with my morning chores, and they went fast. We had the cow milked and the hogs slopped and the dogs fed and the eggs gathered and breakfast down and were on our way to the creek before the dew had even started to dry off the grass. The April rains had washed a new hole in the creek up near the pasture ford and I was anxious to see what was in it. We dug some worms out of the black mud beside the cow barn and set out across the field, the dewy grass soaking our rolled-up overalls to the knees and making our bare feet shine with moisture. We had already cut poles for the year and carried them over our shoulders.

"Man, listen to Runt. He sure wants to go fishing," Simmer said.

It was true. We were already a quarter from the house, but we could hear Runt just as clear as a bell. He was telling us in that almost-grown hound dog voice of his that he didn't appreciate being left at home while we went to the creek.

"You can't take him, though," I told him. "You can't keep him out of the water, scaring the fish. And if you sit down to fish he's got to lick you in the face and paw you to death trying to get petted. I've tried tying him up, but he just hollers 'til you let him loose. Might as well leave him to do his fussing up at the house where he don't mess up the fishing."

"I'm surprised he stays in that pen, big as he is."

That was true. The pen I had Runt in was a rickety one I had thrown together for him as a pup, to get him out from underfoot of Bruisin' Susan. I had seen him try to climb out and I knew it was only a matter of time before he either managed to get over the fence or knock it down. I planned to build him a permanent pen, but hadn't gotten around to it yet.

Suddenly Simmer stopped. "Look there, Kit," he whispered.

I looked. "It's a bull calf. So what?" The yearling bull, his horns no more than three-inch sprouts, lay dozing on the grass in the early morning sun.

Simmer was wearing that mischievous look of his. When I saw that look slowly spreading across his face, I always perked up. Usually it meant some fun was afoot.

But I wasn't sure this time. Simmer handed me his pole and started toward the bull.

"Hey, what are you goin' to do?" I demanded.

"Shh. I'm gonna keep him from getting up." He was tiptoeing forward, easing toward the bull's head.

"You're crazy," I said, but quietly. "He'll kick your brains out!"

Young cattle can be wonderful fun. Once in a while Simmer and I would get the urge for a ride and so would catch a yearling in a corner of the fence somewhere. One of us would hold the calf at bay with a pole, hemming it into the corner while the other quietly climbed the fence and jumped on board. Cattle are hard to ride with their prominent backbones and no mane to hold onto, so these rides were usually short. But they were wild while they lasted. Another way to use yearlings was to grab one by the tail. Usually they would take off at a dead run, pulling the boy riding caboose along at a pace that had his feet hitting the ground only about every twelve feet.

But this was a trick I'd never seen tried. Evidently Simmer was going to jump on the bull's head and try to hold on so it couldn't get to its feet. But every farm boy knows a beef animal gets up rump first, so most of it is up and moving before its head needs to do anything. I didn't see how Simmer could do anything with this one.

Simmer sneaked closer and closer to the bull. It dozed on, unaware that anyone was around. Then Simmer made his jump.

He landed squarely on the bull's head and was scrambling for some kind of grip around it. Instantly the animal came to life with a startled grunt and sprang up faster than I would have thought possible. He was a deep red color with a little white on his face and some white speckles on his belly. He was a square, stocky animal, so solid for his age that my father had already decided to keep him for a herd bull. Simmer was no match for him.

The bull slung Simmer around like a rag doll. I couldn't see how Simmer was keeping his grip with the animal jumping around, slinging its head right and left like a dog shaking a rat. The bull bucked, he spun, he danced sideways, tearing up the moist ground and sending rocks and shreds of sod scattering. Somehow, Simmer hung on. It was unbelievable.

"Let go, Simmer!" I yelled in terror. "Let go, quick!" I threw down the fishing poles and looked around frantically for a club. It was just as well I didn't find one; I couldn't have done a bit of good with it.

"Let go!" I screamed again. Then I saw. Simmer had let go at the very first. One of the bull's little horns was hung in Simmer's overalls. My friend was being whipped left, right, up, down and dragged across the ground backward, but none of it was by choice. I only heard one or two little strangled yells out of him, but his white face showed plainly enough that he was just as scared as I was. His arms and legs flew in all directions. I thought I felt myself passing out, then suddenly it was over.

Simmer and the bull parted company with a jerk. Simmer went flying through the air in one direction and the bull took off in the other. The ground shook with the pounding of the bull's hooves as he galloped away, tail high, across the pasture. If I hadn't been so scared, he would have been a very funny picture, because Simmer's overalls were still hung on his horn, streaming through the air like a banner over the bull's back. The wind blew through them as he ran, filling them out to full size so it looked like the bull was carrying a passenger.

And Simmer was staring up from the wet grass at me, wearing nothing but his linen drawers and the blankest look I've ever seen on a human face.

It took a minute for Simmer to get back enough of the wind that had been knocked out of him to tell me he wasn't dead. As soon as I was sure, I took off trotting in the direction the bull had taken, hoping he hadn't gone too far before the overalls blew off his head. I found them after about five minutes, lying limp and damp on the ground, still and lifeless compared to how they had looked billowing along above the bull.

When I got back to where I had left Simmer, I couldn't find him at first. Then I heard his voice.

"Hey, Kit! Over here!" I turned toward the creek and there he was, waving to me from behind a screen of chest-high bushes on the creek bank. I walked over and handed him his overalls.

"Simmer, are you sure you're all right?" I watched him pull the overalls up and grope over his shoulder for a strap. I thought he still looked a little pale, but his breathing was back to normal and a mild scrape on his forehead was the only wound I could see.

"Yeah, I'm all right. Shouldn't be, though. Jumping that bull was stupid enough that I should have busted my neck." He giggled softly. "I don't believe I'll try that one again for a while."

Easygoing Simmer. He had come close to getting his brains scrambled, and he could still laugh at himself.

We soon forgot the bull incident. The fish were biting and the new hole was one of the best places we tried. The sun climbed toward the center of the sky and a light breeze came up as if to make us more comfortable. Just before it was time to start to the house for dinner, we waded into the creek for a swim.

There's nothing like cool creek water on a warm day. Fishing isn't supposed to be work, but you get hot hiking up and down the creek, climbing banks and fighting through the brush and vines that always bar the way to the best fishing holes. By noon I'm usually ready for a swim. Fishing isn't at its best in the middle of the day anyway.

Simmer is the best relaxer I know, and he can relax especially well in a swimming hole. He'll magically find the spot where it's deep enough to cover his body but shallow enough for his face to stick up so he can breathe. His spot will have enough current so the water stays fresh and cool, but not enough to disturb his rest by edging him downstream. Once when I popped to the surface after doing some underwater exploring I looked over and saw him lying so still in the water that I could could have sworn he was dead. But just then a big water snake came slithering downstream and brushed across his bare foot as it glided over. Simmer wasn't dead.

It seemed like a good time to get out and head for the house. We were just climbing up the steep south bank of the creek when we heard a commotion that set my heart to pounding. It sounded like a dog and a coon fighting.

The racket came from downstream. As quick as I could scramble to the top of the bank I took off running toward the noise. All I could think of was that Runt had managed to escape from his pen and had gotten into trouble. My heart was in my throat and I heard my pulse pounding fast in my ears. It didn't seem real to think of a coon out in broad daylight like this, but I knew I heard a dog and he was fighting something.

I saved a few yards by cutting off a sharp bend of the creek and suddenly found myself on the edge of a high bank again. The water was ten feet below and on the other side I saw Runt on a gravel bar, going at it fang and claw with a big boar coon.

I knew I only had seconds to save my dog's life. He might have been a match for that huge racoon if he himself had been full grown and had some fighting experience. But a nine-month-old pup who had never been in a coon fight was outmatched to start with. Worst of all, they were fighting on the edge of a creek. Coons are excellent swimmers and they'll carry a fight into the water if they can. If one can grab on to a dog's head it can drown him before he can get it off.

Runt and the coon had torn the gravel bar apart. Dark spots of moisture were visible where they had dug up gravel and overturned rocks. I could see bright red splotches of blood, too, on both animals, and here and there on the rocks over which they fought. Back and forth they raged, snapping, clawing, ripping, sometimes darting and slashing at each other, sometimes locking together and rolling over and over amid the coon's squalling and Runt's growls and yelps. I knew it was only a matter of time before the coon retreated into the water, and Runt didn't know any better than to follow it.

I hesitated, but only for a second. I heard Simmer's thudding footsteps as he ran up and stopped behind me. He knew what I was about to do.

"No, Kit! Don't you jump in the water with that coon! He'll drownd you for sure!"

Then I was hurtling through the air, and Simmer's yell and the snarling of Runt and the coon died for a second as the splashing water closed over my head. I felt my feet hit the rocky bottom and bounced up as hard as I could, swimming for the opposite side.

I was looking desperately for a weapon as I reached shallow water and fought my way onto the gravel bar. There was a thick limb of black driftwood sticking out of a rat's nest of washed-up debris. As my hand closed on it I heard splashing over my shoulder. Runt and the coon were in the creek.

Praying that my club wasn't rotten, I ran the fifteen feet that separated me from the fight. Runt had caught the coon in the shallow water, and now the two were wallowing in the creek, biting and clawing at each other in a mass of water and blood and mud and foam. From somewhere I heard a bigger single splash as Simmer jumped in the creek to help me.

Seconds can turn to hours when the chips are down, and they were down now. I didn't feel the rocks of the gravel bar tearing into my bare feet any more than I noticed the water streaming off me and my hair plastered down in my face. All I could tell as I ran was that I would never make it in time. And then Runt and the coon disappeared.

It was no secret where they had gone. Smothered, gurgling growls surfaced through masses of bubbles for a split second before I saw them again, and the coon was astraddle my dog's head. But now I was close enough to strike, and I struck. There was a chance I'd hit Runt with that heavy club, but there was no time to maneuver. Standing waist-deep in the water, I swung the club with all the strength I had. It hit the coon squarely in the back, but though he came out with an unearthly squall, he didn't let go of Runt. I screamed, unthinkingly and uncaringly and struck again. Then I dove for a hold on Runt.

I found his thrashing hind leg with one hand and pulled, still swinging at the coon. I knew my blows were weak and ineffective, but I had to get Runt out of the water now. He might already be dead. Suddenly, I could move Runt. The coon had let go. Frantically I backed out of the water, dragging Runt with me. He was limp.

Then the coon came at me. He was wild with rage, and when he's in that state a boar coon isn't afraid of anything. I had put a few feet between me and him as I dragged Runt backward, but he was closing the gap quickly. It seemed like forever before I finally pulled Runt clear of the water and he lay like a dead creature on the rocks. But there was no time to see to him because the coon had reached the

105

shallows and was now scrambling out of the water toward me. I dropped Runt's leg and stood, heaving and gasping, half blinded with water and panic, as the coon ran at me. I braced myself and tried to pull my wits together enough to swing my club. If I missed, the coon would claw some meat off me before I got a chance to swing again.

But he never got to me. At the instant he left the water, something struck the coon hard from the right side and rolled him over on the gravel. Simmer had come to the rescue.

I'd always said Simmer Downs could throw like a bullet. I've seen him cut a rattlesnake in half with a rock, and he's accurate enough to sometimes take birds off tree limbs. But I don't think he ever made a better throw in his life than the one that saved me from that coon. And I didn't give the coon a chance to collect his thoughts, either. While he struggled to get back to his feet I ran over and kicked him halfway across the creek.

He landed out in the current and I saw that he was floating downstream before I turned, sobbing and coughing to Runt. He lay still as death on the rocks of the gravel bar. I picked him up and stumbled across the gravel to the grass beyond and laid him down gently in the shade of a tree. I was sure he was dead. I touched his eyeball. No response.

"Simmer!" I yelled, hardly recognizing the shrill, wavering voice as my own. "Simmer! Come help me!"

Simmer came stumbling over the rocks toward me. He had been following the swimming coon's downstream progress from the bank, picking up rocks and hurling them at the coon, screaming at it all the while. I didn't know or care if the coon was still alive. All I cared about was Runt.

"Here—hold him up by his hind legs!" Simmer heaved Runt off the ground and held him. He hung limp, his ears and front legs dangling. I wrapped my arms around his chest and squeezed sharply three times. I hoped that would clear the water out of his lungs. "Lay him down!" I ordered, and Simmer laid him on the grass.

I had no idea how a person was supposed to revive a dog, but I followed my instinct. I pushed down on his rib cage with my hand and suddenly let up, hoping that in springing back, the ribs would make the lungs pull some air in. I tried it again, but couldn't see any result. Then I wrapped my hand around the end of his muzzle, clamping his mouth shut and making a tube of my curled fingers. I put my mouth to my hand and blew down the pipe.

I thought I felt his lungs give way as I forced air into him, but I wasn't sure. So much air escaped through my fingers. But when I pressed down on his chest again I heard some breath come out through his nose in a sort of a whine. I blew into him again and pressed it out of him again. Then I touched the pupil of his eye again and he blinked.

Desperately I blew once more through my curled hand into his nose, and this time he exhaled himself. I wanted to cry and laugh and scream, but I was too intent on staring at Runt, praying that he'd breathe again on his own. After a second, he did. Then he did it again, then again, and again. Then he moved one front leg, blinked again, and tried to turn his head to look up at me.

I sat back on the grass and cried. Runt was going to make it. I sat there sobbing minute after minute, creek water running off me and tears streaming down my face, while my dog slowly grew stronger.

Runt coughed a few times, sometimes gurgling as he breathed in and out. But his breathing grew deeper and more regular and finally he struggled shakily to his feet. Then he stood there gasping and retching as he cleared the last creek water from his lungs. His big ears hung down, almost hiding his face as his head drooped low and he fought to breathe normally. He was bleeding from a dozen wounds, but none of them looked deep and none of them caused the terror in me that I had felt when I pulled him out of the water, so very limp and still. All the while, I sat and cried and Simmer looked from me to Runt and back again as if he wanted to help but didn't know what he could do. I didn't know, either. So we all waited together for the sky to stop spinning.

Simmer and I lost another string of fish that day, because turtles ate them while we swam and fought the coon and recuperated. Simmer got his wits back first and went back up the creek to collect our tackle, bringing back the sad news about the contribution we had made to the turtle population. We had had some nice fish on that stringer, but it didn't matter much as we started back to the house, walking slowly and feeling the sun drawing steam out of our clothes.

Within fifteen minutes Runt seemed like his old self, trotting and sniffing at everything and crossing back and forth across the path in front of us as if determined to trip both Simmer and me at least once before dinner.

But Runt wasn't his old self, as I found out the next morning. I had been walking around under a dark cloud since the fight at the creek and only waited overnight to give Runt a chance to settle his nerves before testing him. When I brought him his food at daybreak, I carried the coonskin from the woodshed with me. He heard me rattle it as I walked to his pen, but this time he didn't run out and throw himself baying against the gate. He didn't even come out of his house.

Chapter 10

MORE THAN WE KNOW

I patched up the hole Runt had broken in his pen, but I couldn't find it in me to build him a whole new fence, at least not right away. There was a dark, thick cloud over me that made me not want to try to do anything. It had shaken me, all that had happened since Runt had come along. First the fear of not finding a home for him and maybe having to do away with him. Then the pressure of Daddy wanting me to keep him and me not wanting to, then the decision to keep him for the very reason that he wasn't wanted by anybody else, then wondering if he'd make a coon dog, then all the training which was now wasted, then almost losing him in the fight with the coon, then finding out that his overmatched fight had broken him of hunting coons forever. It was a lot for a boy to squeeze into his head and deal with.

So I did what I sometimes did when I had too much on my mind to carry around. I went up to the dead tree on the hill behind our house. From there you could see a full mile up the creek valley. And sometimes you could see inside yourself, too. I climbed up in the tree and lay back on a huge limb for a while, soaking up the sun. I blinked against its brightness and peered through narrowed eyes into the fathomless blue of the spring sky. A dozen different kinds of birds were singing and the breeze was just strong enough to ruffle my hair a little. A cotton puff cloud drifted oh, so slowly, across space above me. It was the most natural thing in the world to start talking to God up here.

"Lord," I said, "Why do You do the things You do? Why are there so many things I can't see any reason for?" Then I started listing a lot of things I didn't understand, and asked Him to explain them to me. I didn't hear any voice, but somehow as I lay back on the big limb I felt that I was being listened to. So I just started pouring out my heart.

I told God how bad it hurt to be the littlest boy my age around. I told him how badly it hurt to get laughed at when I couldn't win any of the races or wrestling matches. I told Him about Runt and how I'd decided to keep him when nobody else wanted him because he was a runt like me, how I'd worked hard to train him so he could overcome his handicaps and be a good coon dog, and how almost drowning had ruined him as a coon dog altogether. It didn't seem fair. And I told God that.

"It don't seem fair, God," I told him. "I've tried so hard to do right by everybody, and to take up for the underdog. Now I don't have my great coon dog I wanted, and I can't get one because Daddy don't want any more dogs. Besides, I wanted Runt to be my own dog. I don't want another one now. I just want Runt to be a good hunting dog, and now he won't ever be one. I'm not saying You've done wrong, Lord, 'cause I know You know better than I do. But would you please tell me why these things have to happen?"

It was one of those times when life was just too big for me to get a grip on. I didn't want to argue with God; I just wanted to understand. I hoped that if I understood it wouldn't hurt so much. I stayed in the tree for a long time, then I climbed down and lay on my back in the grass for a while. Finally, I got up and walked slowly back to the house.

Mama was hanging out clothes when I came back, so she saw me as I walked into the yard. It was just like her to see with one look that something was wrong.

"Kit, what's the matter, son?" she asked. She stopped working and stood looking at me with a clothespin in her hand.

I didn't lie to her. "It's Runt, Mama." I walked over near the clothesline and sat down on the grass.

"Why, what's the matter? Is he hurt worse than you thought?" She shot a glance toward the woodshed and the dog pens.

"No, Mama, he'll be all right. But I'm pretty sure he won't hunt any more. He was too young to fight that big coon yesterday and I think it soured him."

"What makes you think so?" She started working again, but I could tell she was listening. I told her about testing Runt with his coonskin and how he didn't want anything to do with it.

"Well, that's a shame, Kit. You've worked so hard with that dog."

"I don't understand it, Mama. Why do things like this have to happen? I didn't do anything wrong. I tried to do what was right."

"I know, son. You always try to do what's right."

"So why does this happen to Runt? Why do I get stuck with a dog that won't hunt? It seems like all my life I've ended up on the losing end of the deal. What did I ever do that's worse than anybody else?" I could hear my voice starting to get shaky. I'd have to shut up or I'd start crying again. But when I thought about it all, I was just so disappointed.

Mama stopped working again. Her face looked a little shocked.

"Why, Kit, whatever do you mean 'always ended up on the losing end'?"

I guess I hadn't ever said much about being a runt before, maybe because there didn't seem to be anything anybody could do about it. Probably when I had mentioned it Mama had thought it was just a little irritation and I wasn't taking it too hard. But now I told her how much it hurt not to be able to do things as well as the other boys and getting a hard time from bullies like Eddie Sloan. I told her how scared I was that I'd always be little. When I stopped, Mama looked like she was thinking real hard about something.

"Kit, let's you and me go into the house a minute." So we did, leaving half of Mama's laundry in the basket outside. I followed Mama into the kitchen and she told me to sit down at the table. She walked into the front room and came back with her Bible. She sat down across from me.

"I want to read you something, son." She told me she had just recently been reading Psalm 139 and she thought I should hear part of it. She started reading, and I listened hard, hoping I'd hear something that made sense.

113

The first few verses she read talked about how God knows everything about a person, understands all that happens to him and even knows what he's going to say before he says it. It said that that God holds onto a person and leads him, and that you can't get away from God. All that made sense to me, but it wasn't any surprise. I listened more, thinking maybe there was a key in all this that would open things up for me. Then I heard her read something that grabbed my attention.

"'I will praise thee, for I am fearfully and wonderfully made. Marvellous are Thy works, and that my soul knoweth right well.'" I stopped her.

"Mama, what does that mean?" I asked.

"Well, son, I think the person who wrote this is saying that just like the Lord pays attention to everything that happens to us, He paid attention to the way we were made in the first place. He's saying that it's a wonderful thing, the way God makes a baby and then takes care of him through life. And if we're fearfully and wonderfully made, that means that we were made just right, don't you think?"

I studied that a minute. I didn't see how it was so wonderful that I was made a runt.

"You mean it's right that I'm littler than other boys my age? It don't feel very right."

"Well, Kit, God isn't finished making you yet. You may be big like your daddy when you're his age. But even if you're not, you'll be different than you are now. The Lord still has a lot He wants to do in your life. You just can't judge things by what's happened so far. You've got to believe that you're fearfully and wonderfully made, and that the Lord is still making you."

114

I wanted to believe that, but I was a little scared to. "What if I never get big?"

"Then it means that there is something God wants for you that's more important than being big. God doesn't make mistakes, Kit. So you're not a mistake. God has a plan for you and He's making you the best way to fit that plan."

"But Mama, what good could it do for me to be little?"

"I don't know exactly, son. But the Lord knows. He made you."

I didn't understand all this, but I felt a little better. At least there was more to it than that I was just little. Maybe someday I'd be glad. I didn't see how that could be, but it helped to think that it could happen.

I looked up. "Would it be all right if I'd go down to Simmer's this afternoon? Or you think I ought to work in the garden?"

Mama smiled, and it made me feel good. "You go ahead and play with Simmer. The garden'll keep."

I started out the door, then stopped. I'd thought of something else.

I turned around. "Mama?"

"Yes, Kit?"

"Do you think God cares how Runt's made and what happens to him?"

She smiled again. "Well, the Bible says God watches the sparrows. I'll bet He thinks the world of old Runt."

The walk down the road to Simmer's gave me time to chew on what Mama had read and explained to me. I was fearfully and wonderfully made. That just didn't make sense, but as I thought about it, I thought maybe I could accept it. All that I had to do was believe that God knew something I didn't, and that wasn't hard. There was a lot I didn't know.

All of a sudden, I stopped right in the middle of the road. I stood there with the sun beating down on me from straight overhead. The breeze was warm. From somewhere out in the field a meadowlark trilled. It hit me then that God had made the wind and the meadowlark, just like He'd made me. And they were just right, just like wind and meadowlarks should be. I couldn't begin to understand how He did it, but it was done and done right. That and about a jillion other things, all around me. God had made the gravel of the road, the grass waving in the pasture, the creek sliding underneath the rickety wooden bridge I was about to cross. I started walking again.

When I got to the middle of the bridge I stopped again and looked down into the clear creek water rushing over the rocks below me. Here was a good example of the difference between God's work and man's work. God had made the creek, man had made the bridge. I could have built the bridge, I thought. But I couldn't have made the creek. Only God could do that. And my bridge would rot or get washed away in a few years, while the creek would be there a thousand years from now. That's how much smarter God is than me.

I raised my eyes from the water and looked up into the nearly cloudless blue sky. I'll never forget what I said then.

"All right, God. If You say so." And as I walked on across the bridge, I felt that I had spoken for Runt, too.

Chapter 11

LONG EAR OF THE LAW

I got to Simmer's about an hour before dinner time and found him in the barn, forking manure out of a stall into a wheelbarrow. He looked like he wasn't enjoying it particularly.

"Hey, Simmer." He looked up as I walked in and leaned against the rough wooden partition between stalls.

"Hey yourself, Kit. How's Runt?" He leaned his pitchfork against the wall and wiped his forehead with a bare arm.

"He's all right. Mama cleaned up his cuts and she said she didn't think he'd have any trouble healing up. We're keeping salve on 'em." Then I told him about Runt and the coonskin.

"Aw, shucks, Kit. That's a stinkin' shame, after you kept him when you really wanted a different dog, and we put all that training into him, too." He took his pitchfork again and went back to work.

"Well, I was thinking on that while I walked over here. You reckon we could break him for something else? Possums or something?"

117

"Reckon he might do it. Possum hides ain't worth as much, though. Hey," he said as another thought struck him. "I'll bet this means we don't get our saddle horses and repeating rifles any time soon."

"Reckon not." I had already thought of that, but I hadn't wanted to bring it up because it was bound to discourage Simmer. "But we'll find a way."

"Yeah, we'll find a way." He scraped another forkload of manure off on the wooden side of the wheelbarrow. "But I was hoping," he said, with his slow grin growing on his face, "we'd found a better way to do it than working."

I still felt a little shadow of my dark cloud, but I couldn't help grinning back.

I went to the house and asked Mrs. Downs if I could borrow Simmer for the afternoon. She said it would be all right if his father didn't need him. I had the feeling she had heard about Runt getting chewed up and felt a little sorry for me. I went back to the barn and told Simmer what she'd said.

"Well, we're all right then," he said, "'cause he already said all he needed me to do today was clean out this here stall and these two next door." He nodded to his left.

"I'll give you a hand. We'll get this out of the way and then do something worth doing. Like fishing." I picked up a mattock and began chopping the manure into chunks for him to pitch into the wheelbarrow.

When dinner time came we only had one stall left to do, so by about one in the afternoon we had dug our worms and were on our way up the creek. Simmer's mother had fed us dinner and told us to stay out from underfoot for a while, which meant we could stay gone until evening chore time. That suited us fine, because the weather was warm and we were covered with itchy, dirty dust from cleaning stalls. We needed a soak in the swimming hole.

As always in the spring and summer we had fishing lines in our pockets, so we cut some poles on our way to the creek and rigged them up. I should have brought our poles from the day before, but I hadn't thought of it, what with Runt on my mind and all. We stayed away from the bank of the creek until we were well upstream from any place we had been yesterday. I didn't want to see anything that would remind me of the coon fight. So I set a course toward the place we called the diving hole, up the creek about half a mile from Simmer's house.

The diving hole wasn't where we usually swam because there were other places closer. But it was the best swimming hole of all, because it had a wide pool of deep water and a big sycamore tree that grew out over the water at a slant that made it easy to climb. It was a perfect natural diving platform. We had chopped some of the limbs out of the way so we had a good six feet of thick trunk from which we could dive with nothing in the way. I don't know how high it was above the water, but it seemed like a mile when you were up there looking down. You could see over most of the trees along the creek bank and away across the fields.

We didn't swim at first. We wanted to fish the hole before we got to splashing around and scaring the bass so bad they jumped out on the bank to get away from us, as Simmer said. So we fished and we caught a few, but nothing to brag about. We didn't really feel like carrying fish home anyway, being in a lazy mood, so we turned them all loose as soon as we caught them.

119

I made sure that at the last spot I fished I sat in a sunny place on the bank so I'd be plenty hot when the swimming started. It worked, too, because I was surrounded by bushes and trees that stopped what little breeze there was and within five minutes I was sweating.

"Hey, Simmer," I called quietly. "You about ready to swim?"

He didn't answer, so I didn't say any more. He might be trying to sneak up on a promising spot or already have a big one nibbling that he didn't dare spook. I pulled in my line and wrapped it around my pole, sticking the point of the hook into the wood. Quietly I stood up, waited a minute while the kinks relaxed out of my back and then eased out of the bushes and out on the grass of the pasture. I couldn't see Simmer but after a minute or two I heard him crashing through the brush a few yards away.

"I wanted to try a little hole I found where the bank was undercut," he explained. "It looked like the perfect place for a big largemouth to be a-laying. But I didn't feel like waiting long on him to bite. Let's take a swim."

We were ready for a swim. We were still covered with dirt and hay dust from cleaning stalls, and sticky with the sweat of walking in the sun and scrambling around the creek banks. We were going to get a bath, clothes and all. We climbed slowly out on the leaning sycamore, leaning forward for balance and steadying ourselves by grabbing limbs as we went up. The surface of the water looked an awful long way down. And early as it was in the season, the water was still pretty cold. We stood there a minute, holding a limb apiece and daring each other to go first. Then we heard voices.

"Well, who in the world—" I started, but Simmer elbowed me in the ribs to tell me to be quiet. It was hard to see very far because we were surrounded by tree branches, but through the leaves I caught a glimpse of motion and then heard voices again. It was a wagonload of people, mostly young'uns I thought, coming across the field toward the creek. I knew right away what was going on. It was a Sunday School picnic for a bunch of kids from Merle's Chapel.

I knew Simmer had seen them too, and I knew they hadn't seen us yet. We'd be hard to spot up among the branches, even if somebody looked up, which usually people don't. Simmer was planning something, I could tell. He was peering through the leaves, trying to make out exactly who was coming and how many.

"It's Miss Mary Ann Harlow and her Sunday school kids," he whispered over his shoulder.

Simmer and I liked Miss Mary Ann because she was always friendly to us. She wasn't like a lot of young ladies who are all stuck up and try to keep their parasols between them and any nearby barefoot boys as if they were just too proper to look at anybody with dirt between his toes. Nice as she was, though, we weren't in any hurry to see Bud marry her. Bud had always been around to go hunting or fishing or gigging or camping with us, and we knew enough to know that if he ever did get a ring in his nose, we wouldn't see nearly as much of him. We thought things were just fine as they were.

"Let's spy on 'em, Kit," whispered Simmer.

So we stood there watching, the sun on our heads and the warmth of the smooth sycamore bark coming up into us through our bare feet. There was a whole wagonload of people, mostly kids. But we couldn't see enough through the leaves to tell much. Simmer had another idea.

"Let's give 'em a surprise," he said. "Wait 'til they get close, then let's both scream and jump into the water."

You could always count on Simmer Downs to find a way to make something fun out of any old thing that happened, as long as it didn't take too much effort. We stood there quiet until the wagon got almost to the line of trees and brush that was along the creek bank beside us. When they were close enough that we could hear what the children were talking about and even the thump of the horses' hoofs hitting the sod, Simmer nudged me.

"Now!" he whispered.

We both jumped off the tree trunk at exactly the same second and came out with a scream that would have turned a Comanche's hair white, and I mean we kept it up all the way to the water. We hit with a splash that was a little too loud to suit me, because I had caused some extra noise by landing too much over to the front, almost a belly flop. When the water closed around me, filling my ears with the sizzling noise you always hear when you go under with a bunch of bubbles, the coolness felt awfully good on my stinging skin.

When I came up there was no Simmer, just a mess of bubbles and waves washing up on the gravel on the far side. Then there he was, popping to the top blowing and spitting, his hair plastered down flat in his face. He slung his head, spraying me in the face while he treaded water.

"Listen," he said, panting.

I lay back in the water, floating and paddling under the surface so as not to make any splashing noise. There wasn't a sound from the bunch in the wagon. I could just see them stopped up there, Miss Mary Ann and whoever was driving for her, probably pale faced and wide-eyed from hearing our scream and splash from just twenty feet away when they hadn't known anybody was within a mile. In a minute they'd think to come and check on whoever it was that screamed, but they wouldn't know whether to or not, because sometimes some of the boys didn't take their clothes in with them when they went swimming.

I heard one little voice say, "What was that?" in sort of a quiet way, like whoever it was couldn't decide whether they really wanted to know. Then there was a crackling and stomping in the brush and we heard a man's voice, big and booming.

"Well I might have known! What're you two young scoundrels doing out here, scaring honest people and horses half out of their wits?"

It was Deacon Harlow, Miss Mary Ann's father. He was standing waist deep in the weeds and brush, right beside the base of our diving tree. Harlow was a tall, lean man who stood up straight all the time as if he had a poker for a backbone. He was the richest man in our end of the county, with St. Louis education and ways. He was a pillar of the Merle's Chapel Baptist Church and very respected. Folks said that nobody could go hungry if Deacon Harlow knew about it. Not if they were willing and able to work, or willing if not able. He had been known to stop his fancy buggy in front of the home of a poor old couple, split them a load of kindling wood and carry it in the house with his own hands, and leave a twenty-dollar gold piece on the kitchen table as he left. He didn't smile a lot so he looked rather stern, like he might be a little mean, but the dogs and boys in the neighborhood knew better.

123

"Good afternoon, Deacon," called Simmer, with a big grin. "Nice of you to join us. Come on in for a swim."

The man almost smiled, his eyes crinkling a little above his dark moustache. "Believe I'll pass this time, Mr. Simmer. I'm driving Mary Ann and her Sunday School monkeys down the creek for a picnic. I just stopped by for a minute to see who was being scalped."

Simmer and I looked at each other and giggled.

Then Simmer said, "Did you say a picnic, Deacon? Do you happen to need any help? Kit and me are real good picnickers."

Deacon Harlow frowned thoughtfully.

"Hmm. Well, maybe I could use some assistance. Mary Ann has packed enough food to feed a regiment, as usual, and I suspect her little ones are more in the mood for playing in the creek than eating."

"Oh, yes sir, we can sure help out with that problem," Simmer said seriously. "Always glad to help out a neighbor."

It had only been a couple of hours since we'd eaten dinner, but time didn't seem to matter much to Simmer when it came to helping out a neighbor. I was interested myself, because Miss Mary Ann was known to make a lot of sweets when she took her Sunday School kids out.

The wagon was a big farm wagon with a load of hay in the back for the kids to ride on, and she was loaded to capacity. Little boys in straw hats and girls in pigtails wiggled and squirmed and tickled each other until you almost couldn't tell which kid was which. It reminded me of a bunch of worms when you turn your bait can over.

"Hello, boys," Miss Mary Ann said with a smile as we walked up, dripping. "So that was you in the creek." She

124

had long, light brown hair and big brown eyes that Bud said would make a spaniel cry for envy. I didn't know exactly what he meant, but I had to admit she sure was pretty. It was a wonder Bud had kept his freedom this long.

The kids were all staring at us as if we'd sprouted up out of the ground in wet overalls. Some of them even sat still for a minute.

"Howdy, Miss Mary Ann," we said together. Then Simmer said, "We volunteered to come along with you, Miss Mary Ann. Your father said you might need some help cleaning up dinner—I mean, after dinner."

She smiled again, bigger this time. "Well, it's true we sometimes have food left over. It's a good thing you came along."

I don't believe there's any more room in the wagon, Deacon," Simmer called as Deacon Harlow climbed back up on the board seat beside his daughter. "We can just walk along behind."

"That won't be necessary, gentlemen. You can ride up front, here." He nodded toward the horses. They were two shining brown Morgans, a perfect match and quality-looking.

Simmer and I looked at each other, then he grinned and started climbing up on the near horse while I scooted around to the off side. I could just barely reach the hame on his collar to get a hand hold. Putting my bare foot on the thick leather trace I hauled myself aboard.

We wiggled around until we got our legs underneath the bridle lines so the Deacon could drive. Then off we went, the kids in the wagon chattering and yelling, hoofs thudding on the grass and Simmer and me in the lead on the big brown horses.

Deacon Harlow had the best horses around. They said he had around fifty head because he bred horses for sale as well as using them for work and riding. Whenever I had a chance to go to his farm, I'd climb on the fences and admire the horses in the pastures. It was enough to make a boy's mouth water.

I thought I knew where we were heading, and I was right. There was a spot on the creek just a little ways downstream where both banks were gentle slopes and the water was wide and shallow. There was good grass and some shade trees. A perfect place for a picnic with not much opportunity for little kids to drown themselves.

Deacon Harlow pulled up the horses under the shade of a big elm and stopped. Simmer and I slid off and helped him put on their feed bags and lift the little kids down from the wagon as the bigger ones climbed down the wheels or jumped to the grass.

Miss Mary Ann had done herself proud with the food and even though I wasn't really hungry, the Deacon seemed to take a little longer asking the blessing than was really necessary. There were several big baskets with everything from fried chicken to apple pies and a big brown jug of cold lemonade. The kids were too excited to eat a lot, and in fact left untouched a whole watermelon for which Deacon Harlow had paid a lot of money, watermelons not being in season yet in Missouri and having to be shipped in on the train from Texas. Simmer and I couldn't stand to see such a treat wasted, so we had a contest to see who could eat the most slices. We got so sick we lost track of who was ahead and finally just quit. Finally, the last of the Sunday School kids went off to skip rocks and hunt crawdads in the creek, leaving Miss Mary Ann to clean up while Simmer and I hunted a tree to sit under and lean against while we repented.

I couldn't see myself, but Simmer looked a little green around the gills.

"Ohhh," he moaned. "I don't think I'll ever eat again, Kit."

I was feeling too sorry for myself to have any sympathy for him. I cradled my aching stomach in my arms and wondered why I did such things to myself. But after all, I thought, it's a sin to waste food. I'd just slouch a little lower against my tree and wait for the pain to ease up.

But there's no rest for the wicked. I had just closed my eyes when the first wave of kids came wandering back from the creek. It hadn't taken them long to decide there wasn't anything down there so fascinating that they couldn't leave it for a minute to go see what the big people were doing. They'd been gone about three minutes.

I heard light footsteps coming near then somebody landed on my lap.

I opened my eyes. It was little Rosebud, her cheeks pink from running and one pigtail starting to come unbraided.

"I've already been to the creek, Rosebud. Let's sit and rest a spell instead." Having her on my lap wasn't making it any easier to breathe around the load in my stomach.

"But I want you to teach me how to skip rocks, Kit. Please come to the creek with me, please, please, please!" She shoved against my belly to help herself to her feet, then took my hand and tugged at it until I thought she'd pull my shoulder out of joint. "Come on, Kit. Please, please, please!"

It was no use. Carefully I got to my feet and stood leaning against the tree a minute to get my breath. Rosebud impatiently grabbed my hand again and dragged me over the tufted pasture grass toward the creek. There was a wet spot on the back of her blue cotton dress where she'd sat on my soaked overalls, but she didn't seem to notice.

"Hey, Kit," she said, looking up at me.

"What is it, Rosebud?" I knew what was coming.

"Will you be my beau?"

"No, silly, I won't be your beau. You don't need a beau."

"But Mary Ann has a beau. Bud is her beau."

I reached down with my free hand and gave a tug on her one good pigtail. "Mary Ann is about twenty years older than you, knucklehead. Talk to me in twenty years and maybe I'll be your beau."

She stopped a second and tried to kick me in the shin. I dodged and yanked on her hand, making her stumble after me.

At the water's edge I looked around for some flat rocks. "Now watch this, little knucklehead," I said.

I prided myself on my rock skipping skill. Simmer and I had competed in rock throwing for years and although he could usually beat me in distance and aim, I always won when it came to getting the most jumps out of a rock across water.

Rosebud let go of my other hand and stood back a step. I hitched up my shoulder strap and adjusted my grip on my rock. With a sweeping sidearm slash I sent the rock stuttering across the calm, shallow water in about fifteen hops before it disappeared into the riffles where the pool emptied out into shallow rapids.

Rosebud clapped her hands and squealed. "Ooh, that was a good one, Kit! Do it again, do it again!" She was almost dancing on the gravelly bank. "Throw another one, Kit!"

But I knew better. If I didn't distract her she'd having me skipping rocks all afternoon.

"It's your turn now, knucklehead. Here," I handed her a good flat rock. "You try it."

She closed one eye and screwed up her mouth in concentration. Then she drew back in awkward, little girl fashion and slung the rock in the general direction of the water. It came out of her grasp too soon and did a single slow arch through the air before plopping into the water about two feet from the edge.

"There you go, Rosebud, that was a real good throw," I sweet talked her. "Next time you'll get more than one splash, just like I do. Want to try it again?"

But she was ready for something else. "No, I don't think so," she said. "I want to play hide-and-seek. "Will you play hide-and-seek with me, Kit?" She took me by the hand again and started to drag me away from the water.

"Why, sure I will, Rosie. Uh...let's get the others to play, too. That'll make it more fun." Maybe the other kids would distract her and I could go lie down somewhere in the shade.

Miss Mary Ann was putting the picnic gear back in the wagon. Simmer was still leaned against the tree with his eyes closed, looking very relaxed. He was probably asleep. Miss Mary Ann smiled when Rosebud told her we were going to play hide-and-seek and asked her to call the other younguns. I popped Miss Mary Ann a wink while Rosebud wasn't looking, and she winked back to let me know she understood. She had helped me escape from her little sister before.

"All right, Rosebud," she said. "Let's get everybody together." She wiped her hands on a red checked dish towel then stuffed it into a wicker basket underneath the wagon seat. Then she held out her hand to Rosebud and the two of them started across the pasture down the creek toward where the Deacon and most of the other kids were.

I turned to Simmer and nudged him with my foot.

"Come on Simmer, we've got to go."

He opened his eyes and looked up at me as if it took a lot of energy. "Go? Go where?"

"I don't know. I just need to get out of here while Rosebud's playing with the other kids so I don't have her climbing on me all afternoon. Come on, get a move on. Hurry up."

After a few more nudges Simmer finally groaned to his feet. With a glance back over my shoulder, I saw Miss Mary Ann standing fanning gnats away from her face while talking to her father. Just that quickly Rosebud had disappeared. She was probably among the gooseberry bushes, eating berries and forgetting all about hide-and-seek. Then I felt a tug at my overalls.

"Are you gonna stay and play hide-and-seek, Kit? Is Simmer gonna play, too?"

Rosebud, who had apparently just sprouted up through the grass, was looking up at me with that sunny, open-mouthed smile of hers, eager to play. She didn't wait for an answer, just grabbed my hand in both of hers and swung on it. I looked at Simmer. He was grinning at me.

"Yeah, Rosebud. We're gonna stay and play hide-and-seek a while." I gave Simmer a disgusted look. Too bad he wasn't the one Rosebud always stuck to. "Come on, Uncle Simmer. You're 'it' first."

I figured it would be easy to disappear during a game of hide-and-seek, but Rosebud wanted to share all my hiding places with me. When time came for the fourth round, I had my plan ready.

"Look here, Rosie," I whispered to her as we scattered to hide. "I know a hiding place they'll never find!"

Her big eyes got bigger. "Where's that?" She stopped and looked breathlessly around at the other kids scampering for cover, as if she was scared somebody else would find the place first.

"There's a big hollow chestnut stump in the bushes just the other side of that poplar tree," I said, pointing. "Get in there and keep you're head down. They'll never think to look in there."

She tugged at my hand excitedly. "Well, come on, let's go," she whispered, trying to drag me with her.

"No, no, there's not room for the both of us. You run and jump in there and I'll find me another place. Hurry now, time's almost up!"

It worked. Rosebud took off running, her limp dress flying behind her. I sprinted off in the opposite direction, heading for where I had seen Simmer disappear behind a grapevine-covered tree. With just a little luck we could wade the creek at the shallow place and be in the woods on the other side before anybody looked our way. But I had only taken a few hard-digging strides when a loud squeal from behind stopped me in my tracks. It was Rosebud's voice.

"A snake!" She was yelling. "There's a snake in the stump!"

I spun around and flew across the tall grass toward her. The other kids were springing up from their hiding places among the fescue and behind bushes, craning their necks every which way to see where the excitement was. I nearly tripped over a tousle-headed boy with one suspender when he popped up out of an abandoned badger hole in the grass.

Already I realized that Rosebud hadn't screamed in fear; she wasn't afraid of snakes and in fact loved to play with them, and frogs and lizards too. Her squeal had been one of pleasure at her unexpected find. But whether she was scared or not, I most certainly was. She wasn't old enough to know the difference between the garter snakes Bud and I caught for her, and a water moccasin. She knew not to go near a snake with a rattle, and that was about all she knew about it.

She had just picked up a dead limb and started to poke playfully into the stump with it when I came pounding up and snatched her away. Grabbing her by the shoulders, I jerked her back and dumped her in the grass. Whirling, I picked up the stick she had dropped and looked into the stump. There, curled up among the litter of dead leaves and rotten wood, lay a fat copperhead. His head was up and his wiry tongue flicked out as he tried to figure out how to react to all the commotion. A twitch seemed to vibrate through him underneath the copper diamonds on his scaley skin. He was on guard, alarmed by Rosebud's squealing and poking with the stick. Copperheads aren't particularly timid snakes and I felt a little dizzy at the thought of what could have happened if I had been a second later in getting Rosie out of the way. But there was no time to think of that now. Little kids were running from every direction, it seemed, to get in on the excitement.

"Everybody stay back!" I yelled. "It's a copperhead!"

I knew I had to kill the snake. Already Rosie was scrambling to her feet, which meant in about two seconds she'd be clawing at me and trying to kick me in the shin for yanking her away from her new found pet. And in the time it would take to fend her off and explain, a dozen other little ones could swarm over the stump wanting to see the creature.

I struck at the copperhead with the stick but the walls of the stump kept me from hitting him. So I jabbed the stick into the hollow of the stump over and over, trying to get in a killing stab while he writhed and squirmed and tried to strike upwards. Boys and girls were all around now, most of them keeping some distance as I yelled at them to stay back and poked at the snake. Suddenly the stick broke in my hand and I looked around desperately for another weapon. Any second one of the jumping, squealing children might get too close or the snake, finding itself cornered, might come slithering over the rim of the stump and nail somebody before he could get clear. I jumped toward a head-sized rock just as the boy with one suspender came flying up and crashed into me. He staggered as he bounced off me but managed to stay on his feet. I gave him a hard shove away from the stump as I pounced for the rock. With both hands I raised it over my head then sent it crashing down onto the snake.

Instantly I snatched up the only other handy rock and stood there gasping from running and excitement, trying to tell whether I'd killed the snake or not. Only a loop of his red-brown body and the tip of his tail could be seen

133

protruding from under the rock. As I watched the tail gave a couple of twitches then was still.

"You reckon he's daid?" one of the little boys wondered.

"Yeah, he's dead," I told him. I took a couple more deep breaths. "Tell you what," I said, looking around at the children, "some of y'uns bring me some more rocks and we'll fill up the whole stump over top of him, just to make sure."

They all scattered excitedly, chattering and running in circles.

"Kit, are you all right?" It was Miss Mary Ann's voice.

I turned around. "Yes, Miss Mary Ann. I'm fine. Just a little out of breath, that's all."

Miss Mary Ann stood pale and wide-eyed by Rosebud, holding her tightly by the shoulders. Deacon Harlow and Simmer were beside them.

"Are you sure it was a copperhead?" the Deacon asked.

"Yessir, Deacon Harlow. It was a copperhead, all right. A big one."

He stuck out his big hand toward me. "Then I'm mighty obliged to you, my boy. If that thing had bitten Rose Marie, it could have been very bad. Many thanks."

I shook his hand, feeling good about what he had said, but a little embarrassed, too. Everybody has killed a copperhead at one time or another; I'd just been the closest big person to the goings on.

Miss Mary Ann had to get her two cents in too, as women will do, so she embarrassed me more with a big hug. "You're a hero, Kit," she said, smiling at me.

That made me want to squirm, and it was even worse because Simmer, who was standing behind her and her father, thought it was so funny that he mimicked her silently, mouthing the words, "You're a hero, Kit" soundlessly and then pretending to hug and kiss somebody. I'd find a way to get even with him for that.

Rosebud was confused. "Was that a bad snake?" she asked, looking up at Miss Mary Ann and the rest of us.

"Yes, honey, that was a bad snake," her father answered. "And if it had bitten you, it would have made you very sick. From now on, remember to always stay away from snakes until a big person tells you it's all right."

"Yes, Papa," Rosebud said, and she said it as if she meant it. Which I knew she did, but I also knew she'd forget it the next time she saw a snake. The child was a disaster waiting for a chance to happen.

After we piled the stump full of rocks over the copperhead the hide-and-seek game started up again. It was half an hour before Simmer and I found our chance to sneak away, and then it was only because little Tommy Montgomery dozed off as he lay on his belly in the back of the wagon while counting to a hundred. I wasn't sure I should go slipping off with little Rosebud still on the loose, but I caught Miss Mary Ann aside and she agreed to keep an eye on Rosie so I could leave. So we finally did get away, but not before I had had to tell Rosebud twice more that I would not be her beau.

Once we got clear of the picnic, Simmer and I headed back to the diving hole where we spent the next hour swimming, diving and lazing around. We were lying in the water at the edge of the gravel bar talking about what to do to entertain ourselves until chore time when Simmer had an idea.

"I know what we can do, Kit," he said, sitting up suddenly in the water. "Let's go over to Mr. Wilcock's house and have a look around."

"Mr. Wilcock's house? What for?"

"Just to see if he left anything interesting around. Besides, remember that strawberry patch he had?"

I remembered the strawberry patch, all right. Up until he had died the summer before, old Mr. Wilcock had been known as having the greenest thumb around when it came to growing fruit and berries. Last spring, being old and stiff, he had hired Simmer and me to pick his strawberries in exchange for a third of what we picked. It was lucky for us that he didn't count what we ate while we were picking, because we'd have ended up owing him. His strawberries were the sweetest things I'd ever eaten.

"I don't know, Simmer. I'm still full of watermelon."

"So? It's a half hour's walk to his place. You'll be ready to eat berries by the time we get there."

It was more like only a fifteen minutes' walk to Wilcock's, but I let Simmer talk me into it. We found the place looking abandoned, the house windows boarded up and Mr. Wilcock's famous garden a mass of weeds. But behind the barn the strawberry patch, though overgrown, had more than enough fat, red berries hiding among the weeds to make our trip worthwhile.

It was getting toward evening chore time, so we headed home through the woods at what we called an Indian walk. Indian walking meant we travelled so as to leave as little track behind us as we possibly could. Simmer and I used to practice this to sharpen our skills for the day when we would be old enough to go out west and fight Indians. We'd wade in creek branches, walk fallen logs whenever we could find them, sometimes even climb a tree and jump to the limbs of the tree next to it. We tried to stay out of fallen leaves and soft dirt, winding our way through the driest and rockiest ground we could find. It took twice as long to get anywhere, but that wasn't as important as learning to be good scouts.

We were about a quarter of a mile from the Flat Creek road on our way back to my house when Simmer, who was teetering along a downed log ahead of me, stopped suddenly.

"Look at that, Kit!" He was pointing up.

I looked and whistled. About twelve feet up in a poplar tree there hung the biggest hornet's nest I had ever laid eyes on. It looked as big as a bushel basket, a fat, cone-shaped thing with a gray, papery outside. At the entrance hole in in the bottom of the cone a constant trickle of hornets went in and out.

Simmer looked at me and grinned and I grinned back. "That's a big 'un, Kit," he said.

"Biggest I ever seen."

We sat down on the log to make our plan. One of our favorite games was rocking hornet's nests. You had to be close enough to the nest to bust it with a rock, but far enough away to have a good head start in case the family inside figured out who was shelling their house. Simmer and I had tried it from too close once, mainly because we didn't see any traffic and thought the place was vacant, and ended up getting chased into the creek.

We looked around for the right place to launch an attack before beginning our customary argument about whose turn it was for first throw. It would help to have a downhill slope, clear running room without too much brush in the way. But you needed to be in good throwing position, too. I twisted around on the log to look at the area behind me, then I heard something.

"Listen," I told Simmer.

But when I looked at him he had already heard it too. Something or somebody was moving through the woods in the direction from which we had come. We sat dead still and strained our ears toward the faint rustling of leaves and the occasional popping sound of a dry twig being stepped on. As it came closer, I could tell it wasn't human. There wasn't the cadence of a man's footsteps. It was more of a constant shuffling through the leaves, like a four-footed animal.

We looked at each other. "Deer?" I suggested hopefully. We didn't often get to see a deer up close.

"Nah." He was right. The noise didn't have the crisp, loping rythm of a deer.

It kept getting closer. It was a dog or fox or maybe coyote, pattering through the leaves at a good pace, not being particularly careful to be quiet. So probably not a fox.

But after a second more the sound got close enough that there was no doubt.

"It's a dog," Simmer said out loud. Then about fifty feet away I saw a patch of tan emerge from a huckleberry thicket and become a dog's head. It was Runt!

Simmer and I both yelled then, we were so surprised and tickled that Runt had managed to escape once more and find us 'way out here in the woods. The dumb galoot just wasn't going to be denied a tramp with Simmer and me, even if he could only get in on it late. Now he saw us and threw his nose up to make sure we were who he thought we were. Then here he came, tearing through the brush, long ears flapping, tongue dangling to the side from a big doggy grin. He was happy as a hog in a corn patch.

"Hullo, Runt!" I slid off the log and knelt to greet him, almost getting bowled over on my haunches for my trouble. Runt wriggled and jumped around me as if he hadn't seen me in a year, licking and slobbering in my face and trying to scrape me to death with his big scratchy paws. Simmer flopped on the leaves with us, and then Runt divided his attention betwixt the two of us, whining and growling and yipping and slurping and chewing on any part of us he could get ahold of. We laughed and hollered, rolling in the leaves as we fought him off. Finally Runt was satisfied that he'd given us enough exercise and settled down enough to lie down and chew on my sleeve while Simmer and I patted on him.

"Well, I swanee, Kit," Simmer declared. "I never seen such a dog to get out of a pen and tag along. There's just no gettin' away from him." He rubbed Runt briskly along the loose hide of his rib cage.

"No, I reckon he's just like his pappy. Remember, Sergeant Jenkins said old Buck was an escape artist."

"Yep, he did. Runt must've inherited it. He's just like his pappy," he repeated. Then he said it again. "Just like his pappy. Just like old Buck."

There was something funny about the way he said it. I looked at him. Simmer was looking at me too, and his eyes were wide. Suddenly I knew what he was thinking and I felt my eyes get big, too.

"Just like Buck! Maybe Runt could be a man dog!" Simmer yelled.

"Yeah! We could make a bloodhound out of him! We'll train him to hunt people," I said, all excited. "He tracked us down, didn't he?"

"He tracked us down."

"And it wasn't no easy track, neither."

"It wasn't no easy track, neither."

"He's got the blood in him."

"He's got the blood in him."

"We could catch crim'nals for my daddy."

"Yeah, we could catch crim'nals for your daddy." Then Simmer looked serious. "But I reckon that still don't get us our horses and Winchesters. Too bad you can't skin crim'nals and sell the hides."

That was too bad. We might make a useful dog out of Runt yet, but catching people doesn't give you hides to sell. Then all of a sudden I remembered something and a whole new world opened up.

"Simmer! I got it! We're gonna have them guns and horses yet!"

"How's that?"

"Rewards! Daddy's got a whole drawer full of wanted posters at the office and some of them fellers are worth as much as five thousand dollars! We catch the right one and we can buy every horse and rifle in Missouri!" I felt like laughing and crying and yelling all at the same time.

Then Simmer gave an Indian yell and we both jumped up and started doing our war dance. We cut it short because that got Runt all excited again and he had to help out, jumping and snapping and yelping at us as we hopped around screeching. We sat back on the log and got our breath back while Runt jumped up and leaned his front paws against it between us so we could both have the pleasure of rubbing his head and ears for him.

Simmer slapped me on the back and grinned. "Kit, we'll have to get him a sheriff's badge to pin on his collar."

"Yep," I agreed. I looked into my pup's brown eyes and tugged a floppy ear. "Runt, from now on you're the long arm of the law."

"You mean the long ear of the law," said Simmer, chuckling.

I cackled right back at him, and we sat there for the longest time, petting Runt and talking about our coming adventures as lawmen. And suddenly the dark cloud that had come over me that morning just blew away.

Chapter 12

TRAINING THE MAN DOG

There are lots of good dog men in the Ozarks, but I didn't know of one that knew anything about training a bloodhound. Most everybody broke coonhound or foxhound pups by just turning them loose with the older dogs on a hunt, and then the pack instinct and the urge to chase took over. There wasn't a whole lot for the man to do. But as far as I knew, or Daddy either, there wasn't a trained bloodhound any closer than Buck up at Springfield. So there wasn't a pack to train Runt for us. We'd have to figure out a way to do it ourselves.

That was what had brought Simmer and me to his Grandad Smucker's place this afternoon. We sat on the porch rail of his old unpainted clapboard house and swung our legs while we told him about our plan and he sat on the top step and whittled at the chunk of cedar wood that he kept lying in the flower bed near the porch steps. Runt settled down for a snooze near his feet.

"So you gals want to make that pup into a bloodhound, hah?" Grandad was always calling boys girls and cats dogs; it was one of his little ways of being funny. He spat into the flower bed. "Why would y'uns want to do thet?"

"Because he's soured on coons." I told him about Runt fighting the big boar coon and how now he was scared of even a dead skin.

"Hmmm. Well, no, he ain't likely t' ever make a coondog now. Lot o' pups never git over bein' scared like thet."

"But he's got bloodhound in him, too," Simmer offered. "We thought maybe we could train him to chase people, and then we could help Kit's daddy catch robbers and such, and we could get some reward money."

"We want to get some good horses and Winchester Seventy-sixes so when we're older we can go west and fight Indians," I added.

Saying it to a grown-up person, it almost sounded a little childish, like when I was little and dreamed of being a knight and killing dragons. But Grandad Smucker never showed a trace of a smile.

"Fight Injuns, hah?" He spat again, narrowly missing Runt's head. "Well, better you th'n me. That there's dang'rous work, they say. But now, I ain't never trained a dog to hunt people. I've trained coon dogs and squirrel dogs and fox dogs and stock dogs, but now how y' go about trainin' a man dog, I wouldn't know. Didn't that prison feller say nothin' 'bout how they done it when he was down here last summer?"

"He said they started 'em off as little pups just a few weeks old," I told him. "Said you play with 'em a minute, then run off a few steps and they'll chase you. Then you fight around with 'em a little more, and run off a little farther. Said you just start with that and work 'em up a little at a time 'til they'll chase you even when they can't see you and have to start using their nose. We did something kind of like that with a fresh coon skin when we broke Runt to hunt coons."

"Uh-huh." He whittled a few more strokes. "So have y' tried thet any more since y' d'cided to make him a man dog?"

"No, we wanted to talk to you first so we didn't maybe do the wrong thing."

"Hmmm. Well, sounds t' me like you're on the right track. He's still young 'nough to want to play a lot, ain't he?"

"Yessir."

"Then my guess'd be that's the way to go. He tracked you t'other day 'cause you're his pal. I 'spect he could be trained to track other people, too. Y' might try startin' with Simmer since he's kind of a pal too, havin' Simmer run off a little ways with a piece o' bacon or somethin'—let the dog smell the bacon first so's he knows he's got it—then turn the dog loose and when he catches up with Simmer, he gets the bacon. Or liver, or whatever y' got that he likes."

Simmer and I looked at each other. "That makes sense," Simmer said.

Grandad went on. ""I b'lieve it'll work to get him a-chasin' you, Simmer. Now, to get him to chase a stranger might be somethin' else. But I b'lieve if you use the meat he'd do it."

"Wouldn't that make him not want to chase anybody that didn't smell like meat?" I asked.

"I don't hardly b'lieve it would. Seems like maybe oncet he got it into his head that people were somethin' to chase, bein' a hound dog he'd just have it in him to chase 'em.   Might depend on how much of him thinks bloodhound and how much thinks coon dog. I jest dunno."

"Sounds like it's worth a try, Kit," Simmer said. "Let's find some bacon and see."

Grandad pointed across the barn lot with the point of his pocket knife. "Cut yerself a few slices off'n thet side o' bacon in the smokehouse yonder. We got aplenty of it."

"Thanks, Grandad," said Simmer. "We'll let you know how it works out."

"Yeah, thank you sir," I said. "'Bye." I whistled to Runt. "Come on, boy."

Grandad kept on whittling but said, "S'long, Kit. S'long, Simmer." Then as Runt trotted past, "G'bye, kitty."

When we got back to my house we put Runt in his pen, hoping that would make him more excited to run and play when the time came. An hour later we took him out and tied a rope to his collar. I wanted to try tracking without the bacon first, so we had left it in the house and washed our hands with warm water and even soap, hoping to get rid of most of the smell. First Simmer held Runt and I took off running around the corner of the barn, calling to him and clapping my hands just like I did when I wanted him to play. I looked back over my shoulder and Runt was lunging and fighting, trying to slip his collar so he could chase me. I went on past the garden and hid in the tall grass at the edge of the pasture beyond. I could hear Runt whining and yelping, struggling to let loose.

I hollered, "Let him go!"

When Simmer yelled, "Here he comes," I ducked down in the grass. I didn't hear anything more for a minute, then Runt was pounding his big feet along the garden path, sounding like a running plow horse. He hesitated a minute, whining, at a place where I had started to turn off the path and then changed my mind, as if he wasn't sure what I had done. Then I heard the familiar sound of his snuffling and snorting and I knew he had gone to ground scent to find me. The next moment he shoved through the few feet of tall grass between me and the tomato patch and jumped all over me, wriggling and licking, his crooked hound's tail whipping with joy.

I sat up and whooped. "Way to go, ol' Runt! Good job, boy!"

I don't know who was more excited, Runt or me. But he had to do more than just hunt me; I already knew he would do that. The next step was to get him to chase someone else.

Runt was at my heels when I ran back to Simmer in the yard.

"Did he do it?" Sim wanted to know.

"He did beautiful," I told him. "Let's see if he'll chase you now."

"All right. You want me to get the bacon?"

I thought a second. "Naw, let's try it without first, just to get an idea what he'll do."

So this time I held Runt while Simmer ran off, whooping and shouting and calling to Runt. When I heard him call that he was hidden, I turned Runt loose.

"Go get him, boy! Find him, Runt!" I was yelling and jumping up and down, trying to act real excited so maybe Runt would be excited, too.

He took off after Simmer, disappearing behind the barn as I hollered and yelled encouragement. But then he was back, whining and pawing at me and wanting to play. It seemed that he wanted to chase Simmer, but he didn't want to let me out of his sight for fear I'd hide from him again.

So I yelled, "Find him, Runt!" again and took off after Simmer myself. In just two jumps Runt had passed me and was pounding around the far side of the barn, nose low and ears flying. Once back there, of course, I had no idea which way Simmer had gone. But I didn't need to know; Runt was already plunging off the garden path and into the grass opposite the way I had gone before. Into the woods by the pasture he went, and I had no sooner ducked under the low limbs of the first tree than I saw Runt rearing up on a big oak, scratching at the rough bark with his paws and whimpering and yelping for all he was worth. Just out of his reach Simmer crouched on a limb. He dropped to the ground and went to rough-housing with Runt. I ran to join them and praised Runt for his good job.

"Looks like we got him started, Kit," Simmer congratulated me.

"It sure does," I answered, pounding on Runt affectionately. I was tickled to death. "Next step is to get him to chase somebody he don't know, but I bet he'll do it. He chased you just for the fun of chasing. I'll bet if we use bacon just once in a while, he'll hunt anybody we put him on."

"Sure he'll do it. I'll get Bobby to run for us next, then we'll think of somebody he's never even seen before and see how he does. We can use the bacon if we need to at first, but I'll bet he takes right to it."

And that's just how it worked out. In the weeks after that, we hunted not only Bobby but practically every other kid within five miles. Once in a while we'd have the kid carry a piece of bacon or some other meat for a treat for

Runt, but he seemed to love tracking just for the sake of the chase. I don't know if it was Buck's blood in him or if it's just the nature of a hound to hunt, but Runt looked like a pup determined to outdo his daddy or die trying.

Runt had the nose for it, too. As he got more experienced, we made the trails harder, with more twists and turns and back tracks. We gave the runners more and more time before starting Runt. But as he matured he just kept getting better and better. Once in a while Simmer would leave one of the tricks Sergeant Jenkins had taught us in the trail, and sometimes Runt would be confused for a while. But between his nose and my visual tracking, we would get it straightened out sooner or later.

The one time during that summer that Runt failed to run his quarry to ground was for a reason I had never looked for, and one that gave a hint of possible trouble to come. Simmer and I had bribed Bobby to lay a track running from their chicken house down along the creek and around a sink hole called Oliver's lake, then back to their barn. It's swampy and brushy around that sinkhole, and Bobby wasn't excited about having to fight his way through all that. But half a stick of peppermint candy put a different light on the deal, and we finally talked him into it.

"Just a minute," he said as he left us on front porch with Runt. "I've got to go in and get my mountain man hat. I'll go out the back door."

"He's sure proud of that new hat," Simmer told me as we turned to sit down on the steps and wait. "Daddy made it for him last week and he's wore it everywhere but to bed."

I only half heard him. My mind was on Runt and the progress he'd made this summer. He was over a year old, not as big as a normal hound but as big as he'd ever get. He seemed sold on the idea of tracking people now, and it didn't matter if they were friends or strangers; he just had to stick his nose in the dirt and hunt them. I thought he was ready to go for real game, but Barry County had the sad habit of being a quiet place. So far, Daddy hadn't had to call on us to chase so much as a watermelon thief. I'd never thought I would live to regret seeing Bernie Sloan move away, but I almost regretted it now.

Simmer and I had cut up some old leather plow lines to make a harness for Runt. I hoped I could train him to track slowly enough so I could keep up with him, but he surely wasn't there yet. So we had made the harness for him, trying to remember how Buck's harness had looked, and putting some buckles in so that it could be adjusted as Runt grew. We worked him with a twelve-foot strap snapped to a ring on his back and that gave me enough slack to go around most of the briars and thickets and still have time to catch him as he came out the other side. I had told Simmer that when Runt earned our first reward for an important manhunt, I planned to take him to a harness maker and replace his old harness with a fancy new one, complete with silver shiny things like Bud Carson had on his saddle. Nothing was too good for Runt.

"You ready to go?" It was Simmer, breaking in on my daydreaming.

"Huh? Oh, yeah. Let's go find Bobby." I stepped off the porch and picked up Runt's strap. "Come on, boy, let's go huntin'."

The minute I grabbed the leash, Runt knew what was happening. In a flash he was on his feet and jumping around the yard, sniffing air and ground for a hint of what he was supposed to chase. I dragged him around the corner of the house and across the back yard, followed by Simmer. "Find him, Runt!" I said about the time we crossed the path from Simmer's back door to the garden gate.

Runt didn't have to be told twice. He smelled Bobby on that path, and he knew Bobby had walked out of the yard and not come back. He lunged toward the gate, snuffling and scrambling, dragging me along. Along the edge of the garden we went, until we hit the fence where Bobby had climbed over into the lush grass of the hayfield that bordered the creek. His trail was plain as day even to the eye.

I handed the strap to Simmer and he held the plunging Runt until I got over the fence, then I took it back and we were off at a run. The trail was only half an hour old and Bobby couldn't help rubbing against lots of grass and weeds. He had left a thick trail of scent for the dog. In fact, it was an easy track for Runt. But today it wasn't my purpose to challenge my dog with an old trail. I wanted to give him a good hot track to keep his excitement level up. Also, we were going through some rough terrain and brush in hopes of toughening Runt and ourselves for anything we might ever face tracking criminals.

"He's running good, Kit," I heard Simmer say over my shoulder.

"Yep, he's hot as a two-dollar pistol," I replied.

And Runt was looking good. He forged along through the tall grass, trotting fast and keeping plenty of tension on the strap, towing me along. His head stayed down in the thick scent, with none of the swaying side to side that you see when the trail is faint and the dog is having to look around for fragments of it.

150

Again we came to a fence, this one separating the hay field from the cow pasture. Once across the pasture, we'd have one more fence to cross into the brushy land along the creek. Once more I handed the strap to Simmer who stood panting, leaning back against the force of Runt on the other end. I vaulted the top rail of the fence and took the strap back.

Bobby's trail was harder to find now, even though it was fresh. There was a light breeze blowing, and that always scatters scent. The grass was grazed down short so there was little to rub against a boy's clothes and hold scent. Besides, cows were using the pasture and they leave a lot of smell. But Runt plowed straight ahead, slowing down a little and whuffling along with his nose tight to the ground as he sorted things out.

It was only a couple of minutes' tracking across the pasture and quickly we found ourselves approaching the fence on the far side. Runt was sure of himself now, picking up speed and dragging me along like a fast plow mule. Then we were at the fence and I shortened up on the strap. I glanced over my shoulder to see if Simmer was close enough to hold Runt so I could climb the fence. Runt was already forcing his way through a small gap between the middle rails.

Suddenly my dog gave a loud yelp and leaped back as if he'd been shot. He nearly knocked me off my feet in his terrified attempt to get clear from the fence. I gave out with a surprised yelp myself. I felt my heart hammering as I scrambled to collect the sudden slack of the strap and pull Runt close to me.

"Land sakes, what's happened, Kit?" Simmer demanded.

"I think he's been snake bit," I said. Panicking, I knelt beside Runt and tried to examine him. He was quivering all over and cowering against me. "It's all right, boy," I said, trying to calm him even though I was shaking myself. "Here, let me have a look at you." But there was no sign of snakebite, none of the sudden swelling that usually marks the site of penetration. I looked and felt all over his face, shoulders, forelegs, all the places a dog usually suffers a snakebite. There was nothing.

I looked up at Simmer. He had advanced cautiously to the fence with a rock in each hand, peering into the brush and weeds on the other side for a glimpse of what had hurt or frightened Runt. Suddenly he grunted and dropped the rocks. I stood up beside Runt, still patting his head to calm him. Simmer leaned far over the fence and plucked something I couldn't see from the prickly grasp of a blackberry briar.

"I b'lieve this is what scared him, Kit. I should have thought of it before. Bobby must have lost it climbing the fence."

He turned and held it out to me, the thing that had so terrified Runt and the reason he would do no more tracking that day. It was Bobby's new mountain man hat.

A coonskin cap.

Chapter 13

HIGHER EDUCATION

Simmer came down with the measles the next day, so it was several days before he felt up to going back to Grandad Smucker's to talk to him about Runt's problem. It wasn't much help when we did, because the only thing Grandad could think of to do was to kill a coon and keep its hide lying around where Runt would get a distant sniff of it every day until he got used to the idea that it wouldn't hurt him. He said he still didn't think Runt would ever hunt coons again, but that if he smelled the smell often enough he'd finally not pay much attention to it.

I wasn't bothered by the fact that Runt would never be a coon dog; I had gotten used to the idea and anyway Simmer and I both thought it would be a lot more interesting to hunt outlaws than varmints. Everybody hunted varmints.

But as I said, Grandad's advice wasn't much help right away. It was spring, the mama coons had babies and I didn't want to trap or shoot one when it might turn out to be a female and leave orphans. So we just went ahead and worked Runt and he kept tracking better and better. The only problem was that once in a while, especially around the creek, he'd run across a heavy coon scent and get to acting nervous and confused. I never had him quit on me again as he had when he ran into Bobby's coonskin cap, but sometimes I had to walk him well past a muddy bank where I saw fresh coon tracks with the hand-like prints of its forepaws and start him again.

But if I couldn't deal with the coon problem, Simmer and I found plenty of other things we could do to advance Runt's education. We kept increasing the length and difficulty of the trails we worked him on, and he began to show us that he was going to have a good cold nose, the kind that could take a trail several hours old and work it on out. That was important in those days because transportation was slow and a lot of time could go by between a crime and the time we could find out about it and get there with Runt.

I don't think Daddy took me very seriously when I first told him Runt was going to be a man dog. But he got to laughing out the other side of his face when I finally talked him into laying a few tracks for us. By the middle of that summer, Daddy could take an hour's headstart and use every woodsman's trick he knew and still not get away from us. Between my skills and Runt's nose, even he had to admit we were a team to be reckoned with.

One trick I wanted Runt to know, one that not even old Buck could do, was to take a person's track and stay on it even if he came across a fresher track of somebody else. I thought that might be important, because there was no telling when we might have to track somebody in town. Besides, Sergeant Jenkins had said that one of the common problems for a dog man was that often the crime scene was stomped over by a bunch of law officers and curiosity seekers before the dog could get there. He had said that usually Buck would stay with the right track if it was fresh enough, but that he couldn't always tell which track to start on. "Scent discrimination," I think he had called it.

Daddy was the one who finally came up with the answer for that one. It was at supper one evening late in the summer. Mama had invited Bud out to eat with us; she felt sorry for him because he had to eat his own cooking so much of the time. She was right; I had sampled some of Bud's Texas jailhouse chili and it was enough to burn a hog's gizzard out. Simmer was with us too, so Mama had cooked a big beef roast and made it a really special occasion.

As soon as Daddy raised his head after the blessing, I made sure the conversation got started off right.

"Daddy, do you know how I could teach Runt scent discrimination?"

He picked up a two-pronged fork and a carving knife and went to work on the roast. "Scent what?" he said.

"Scent discrimination," I told him. "Least, I think that's what Sergeant Jenkins called it. So your dog can tell what man you want him to track if there's more than one man's scent on the scene."

He lifted a slice of roast and scraped it off on Mama's plate, then sawed off a thicker hunk for Bud. "Well, son, I never thought about it. Would be a handy thing for a dog to know, though. Lots of times there's the smell of several people around the scene of a crime. That enough, Bud?"

Bud said it was fine, and Daddy turned to Simmer's plate.

"Like two years ago when that store in Monett got broke into," he went on. "I didn't have a dog, but if I had it

155

would have been right rough for him. The owner came to open up the store at eight in the morning and found a back window busted out and some stuff missing, including all the money from the cash box. I didn't get word and get up there to investigate till that afternoon and by then the smell of the suspect was all mixed up with the smells of the owner and several customers and no telling how many passersby. Would have been hard to tell the dog which track to run."

"Could you have maybe picked up the thief's track a ways from the store?" Bud asked. "Any way to tell which way he'd gone?"

"Maybe so. There was tracks leading from the busted window straight back to the gully behind the store. Might could have started a dog there."

I thought for a minute. It sounded like something Runt and I could have worked out. But it would sure be handy to be able to somehow tell your dog which man was which.

"Didn't Sergeant Jenkins say that some bloodhounds are trained to sniff something with a person's smell on it and then look for that one man's smell?" I asked.

"I believe he did, come to think on it," Bud put in. "But you're not always gonna have a shoe or bandana or something with the scent. Unless you can find something at the crime scene you're sure he touched. Or maybe a visible track you could stick the dog's nose in."

The talk went on that way through most of supper and that suited me just fine. Of course Mama didn't find much in it for her, hound dogs not being something most ladies get excited about. But with Bud there she got so many compliments on her cooking that by the time she was dishing up the blackberry cobbler I could see she had enjoyed supper about as much as I had.

Between the four of us men, we concentrated a lot of brain power on it, and finally Daddy said he thought the thing to try would be having two people lay a track together, then split up. I'd give Runt a smell of something with one person's scent on it when we started tracking them and at the point where the trail split, then make sure he split off the right way. There was plenty of daylight left after supper, so Simmer and I made Daddy and Bud come outside and get started. Bud groaned as he pushed back his chair.

"Dadburn it, Kit," he complained. "Seems like you could let a boy set a minute and let his supper settle 'fore you go chasing him round the countryside."

"If I do that you'll sprout roots and I'll never get you busted loose from the porch," I told him with a grin. "Just take your medicine like a man."

He and Daddy both griped as I drove them out of the house but Mama told them no more coffee until they'd helped me and Simmer out.

We agreed that Daddy and Bud would walk together out into the pasture across the road for a hundred yards. Then they would split off and each go fifty yards more and lie down in the grass. Bud would leave me his bandana to start Runt off and drop his hat at the point where he and Daddy split up.

Runt hadn't been out of his pen all day, and when we went around back to get him he was fit to be tied. He was reared up against the gate of his pen, nose toward the sky and baying for all he was worth. Susan and the two young coon dogs were singing harmony, running back and forth

157

and hollering to be let out, but they just had to stay put. I took Runt's harness from the fence where I had hung it and squeezed into the pen with him, wrestling him into his leather before he could lunge past me and take off on his own.

At the edge of the pasture we stopped and looked to make sure our runners were hidden. Then I pulled Bud's bandana from my pocket and rubbed it in Runt's face.

"That's him, Runt! That's the man we want! Find him!" Simmer and I both hollered and jumped around, trying to get him excited about the bandana, and Runt did grab it in his teeth and yank it out of my hand before spitting it out to go snuffling desperately around in the grass for a track.

It was just a second before he hit their trail and swung hard to his left out into the pasture. "Here, Simmer. Grab hold and help me." I handed him the end of the strap. When Runt was fresh and strong like this it was more work than I wanted, trying to hold him down to walking speed. Off through the pasture grass we went, yelling encouragement to Runt and almost being dragged off our feet in return.

Bud's cream-colored Stetson was easy to see against the green background, so I jumped ahead of Runt and snatched it up before he could get to it and mangle it with his big paws. Then I stopped him and waved it in his face.

"Good boy, Runt! Find him!" I shouted. Then I let him go on again.

Just as I thought, he veered off to the right, plowing down Daddy's track. I had made Bud the target of the chase because I figured Runt, knowing Daddy better than Bud, would tend to go after Daddy. He had no sooner made the turn than I popped him a smart one on the rump with the end of the thick leather strap and jerked him to a stop. "No!" I hollered, then dragged him back toward Bud's track. "Find him!" And I shoved the bandana in his face again.

When he hit Bud's track again he took off like a champion and Simmer and I loaded him as he ran with so much sweet talk it would have made me sick to hear anybody else talk to a dog that way. But we wanted him to know he had done a good thing to leave the one track and follow the other, and it looked like it was working. When a minute later he found Bud he like to have clawed the man's clothes off.

"Here, take it easy, you big horse," Bud laughed, standing up from his hiding place suddenly to protect himself from Runt's paws and tongue. "Kit, you didn't let him eat my Stetson, did you?"

"No, I watched out for it," I said, handing it to him. "Old Runt did all right, don't you think, Bud?"

Daddy was there then, striding across the grass with his long-legged shuffle. He had been standing still watching the show since we had put Runt back on Bud's trail.

"You know, Kit, I believe a few more exercises like that and the old boy might just get the picture."

"Yeah." I knelt beside Runt and gave him a hug, ducking my face away from his yard-long tongue. "We'll work him some more. I think this trick might do it."

And we did work him some more. But it's a lot less convenient to find two people to lay track than it is to get one, so it wasn't often we could do it. As the summer went on Runt seemed to be getting the idea, but as it turned out, when the big test came I wasn't at all sure he was ready.

Chapter 14

LOST CHILD

I just couldn't believe that Rosebud was in trouble again.

I reckon that's why I didn't take it more seriously when the Harlow's farm boy, Jory, came galloping down Flat Creek road on one of the farm's blooded horses asking all the neighbors to be on the lookout for a little girl in pigtails. I heard later that some of the other folks around had taken it pretty lightly too, which is not surprising if you know Rosebud well enough to know that she's always wandering off somewhere. Daddy used to say that it was a full-time job for Deacon and Mrs. Harlow and Miss Mary Ann just riding herd on Rosebud.

I knew of my own experience that she was that way. At age three Rose Marie Harlow had drifted into the hog pen at feeding time and nearly gotten trampled for her trouble. At four she had found a ground hornet's nest that everyone else had missed and had managed to collect enough stings that she had to be wrapped in sheets and cold mud for a day and a night. Also at four she had chased "a bird with a pwetty yellow belly" out into the fields and had gotten lost for several hours. At five she had disappeared at a church picnic and had most of the church searching for her in desperation before she was found asleep under a lap robe in one of the buggies. She was six the summer I had to rescue her from a copperhead she was trying to adopt. If trouble didn't follow her around, then she must have been looking for it intentionally.

So, as I say, it was no big news when Jory reported that she had turned up missing again that afternoon in October. I figured she had made a new hide-out in the hay loft or some such thing, and couldn't give it away by answering when she was called. In spite of that, though, I felt a little gnawing uneasiness. Some of Rosebud's adventures had been dangerous.

I stood out front of our house a minute as the hoofbeats of Jory's horse died away in the direction of Simmer's place, idly swinging the yard gate, listening to its rusty protests and thinking. Then I turned and whistled to Runt, who was snoozing on the porch.

"C'mon, Runt." He lazily heaved himself to his feet and followed me around back where I shut him in his pen. I had found that shutting him up for a while seemed to make him more eager to work when he got out. Probably nothing was going to happen, I told myself, but it never hurts to be careful.

I did the evening chores early and was just dropping the latch of the feed crib door when Simmer showed up. I noticed right away that he was wearing shoes even though it had been a warm day. He was ready for anything.

"Hey, Kit."

"Hey, Simmer."

"Hear Rosebud Harlow's wandered off again." He looked concerned and excited at the same time. "Think your pap'll have you and Runt look for her?"

I picked up the empty slop bucket and walked toward the house, frowning.

"Prob'ly not. Prob'ly they've already found her in the hen house playing with the chicks."

"Yeah, prob'ly. She's always going off exploring."

I stuck my head in the door to let Mama know Simmer was here so she could set an extra plate, then we sat on the front steps, not talking much, as if we were waiting for something to happen. Mama called us for supper and we each downed our fair share of fried chicken and mashed potatoes. Then the something happened.

Mama must have been expecting it, by the way she went ahead and fed Simmer and me without waiting for Daddy to get home. When we heard the clatter of a racing horse ending in a scatter of gravel out front, she was the first one to the front door. Bud Carson was looping his reins around the gatepost and starting up the path to the porch.

"Evenin', Miz Hunt," he said, always polite. "Sheriff said to tell you he won't be home to supper. The little Harlow girl hasn't showed up and he's organizing a search party." He turned to me. "Kit, he said get Runt in the wagon and get to Harlows' as fast as you can. He'll talk to you there."

I looked up at Mama, and her face was as white as mine felt. But she nodded, and Simmer and I left the porch by the south side, not using or needing any steps. We had Runt in his harness in a minute, but were just starting to hook up Henry and Henrietta to the wagon when we heard and then saw Bud fogging it back toward town. I knew why he was in a hurry. It wasn't just his job; it was his sweetheart's baby sister.

Mama was on the porch when we drove around the corner of the house headed for the road. "Kit," she called. "Tell your daddy I'll fix some food and be along in the buggy in a little bit."

We never slowed down. "All right, Mama. I'll tell him." Then we were in the road and Simmer was slapping the lines on the horses' backs.

"Hyah! Giddap, you crowbaits!" he hollered, and they got up. I had asked Simmer to drive so I could give my attention to Runt. I also wanted freedom to think.

This must be a bad dream; it was all wrong. Our first chase was supposed to have been after some outlaw, a desperate killer or bank robber with a thousand-dollar price on his head. We were going to collect a big bounty and be heroes and use the reward money to buy cat-stepping horses like Bud's and a new Winchester apiece. None of our daydreams featured a lost little girl, especially a girl who was just like a little sister to me. Not a little girl who loved and was loved by everybody she knew and who didn't have sense enough not to play with snakes. This just couldn't be real.

But it was. There was nothing dream-like about the crisp October afternoon, the dry cool air that now was a rushing wind through my hair. The bits of gravel flying up and hitting us from the horses' feet were hard and sharp and the cloud of dust that billowed behind us was coating the roadside leaves with real powder. It wasn't a dream and I couldn't just wake up from it, much as I would have liked to.

Henry and Henrietta had covered some miles at a very unaccustomed speed when our wagon slid, rattling and spraying gravel, into the yard of Deacon Harlow's place. It was an impressive farm, with sleek, well-bred horses and cows grazing behind tight, solid fences that stretched across hundreds of acres of fields and woods. The house was large and comfortable, a sprawling ranch-style home nestling among big old oak trees. The barns and outbuildings were well-kept, some of them even painted.

But the place looked different this evening. The barn lot was full of saddle horses and wagon teams. A number of other animals were tied to the fence. People milled everywhere, the men talking in low tones and the women mostly in the house or on the long front porch. I could see a knot of them around Mrs. Harlow and Miss Mary Ann, who were sitting in the porch swing with their arms around each other. Bud was standing in the middle of the cluster, his Texas hat looking out of place among the bonnets, patting Miss Mary Ann on the shoulder and telling her we'd find Rosebud. Miss Mary Ann in turn was comforting her mother, who looked like a fifty-year-old Mary Ann and was holding a wadded-up handkerchief in her face as if to keep her head from falling off. I thought I knew about how she felt.

Preacher Snodgrass, hat off and bald head shining like a beacon, stood quietly off to the side of the porch. It was like him to be where anybody had trouble and might need encouragement. I'd have been willing to bet he had been one of the first ones there.

Simmer brought the winded horses to a halt by the barn lot fence as my father, followed by Deacon Harlow, saw us and started over. The groups of men respectfully paused in

164

their talking as the two strode by and young'uns of assorted ages and descriptions scattered like chickens from their path. I guided Runt with his strap as he jumped out the back of the wagon, then I turned to face them.

"Kit, you boys and Runt all right?" Daddy looked serious.

"Yessir, Daddy. We got here as quick as we could."

"Good men. Simmer, can you stick with us if we're here awhile this evening? I know Kit likes to have you along when he tracks."

"Yes sir, Sheriff Hunt. Daddy knows where I am and he said he'll be along after while hisself." I could tell Simmer was nervous, too. Usually he just called Daddy "Mister" Hunt.

Deacon Harlow stepped forward and put his hand on my shoulder. His face looked pale, but he carried himself with the same dignity he always showed.

"Kit, I know you've worked hard with your dog." That was true; we had worked Runt some on his land. In fact, a couple of times Runt had chased a giggling Rosebud from hiding place to hiding place among the barns and sheds. "I want to tell you that I have complete confidence that you can find Rose Marie."

Then he shook my hand firmly, just as he shook hands with the men at church. He shook Simmer's hand, too. Then he turned and walked back across the yard and up on the porch to stand beside his wife. I don't know about Simmer, but he left my insides a boiling pot of feelings. I felt some proud, that the Deacon had confidence in me, some worried, because I knew the thousand-and-one things that can happen to throw a dog or human tracker off a track, and some of a whole passel of other feelings that swarmed around my innards along with the flock of several hundred butterflies that were already there.

I could see the wisdom of Daddy's staying at the Harlow's rather than coming home to get Runt and me. If he hadn't been there, some of the crowd of men and boys would already have fanned out across the countryside, trampling out any trace of scent Rosebud might have left. No doubt Deacon Harlow and some of his farm men had already done some damage. Now Daddy turned to the crowd to give some last-minute orders. He was using his sheriff voice, but not full volume.

"All right, everybody, please let me have your attention." All over the yard conversations switched off suddenly, leaving no sound in the air but the sniffling and whimpering of Mrs. Harlow on the porch. "To keep from making it hard for the tracking dog, I need everybody to stay right close to the house here until we get on a good solid track. That goes for children, too. I'll need a couple of wagons on the road with some blankets, drinking water, bandage material and extra coal oil for lanterns. I need any extra lanterns anybody can spare. I'll also need some rope in case we have to climb any bluffs. I'd like four or five men in the wagons and maybe half a dozen on horseback for searchers and to carry messages. All of you, stay on the road and in a wagon or on horseback to keep from tracking your scent around too much. Right now I'd like somebody to ride into town and see if the doctor is back and if he is, ask him to come out here and stand by in case we need him. As soon as the dog has picked up a track and carried it a quarter of a mile or so, I'd like some of you men to scatter out and cut us some pine knot torches. Some of you ladies might want to cook up some food since there's no telling how long we'll be out tonight. And keep a pot of coffee hot." He looked around the group. "I want to say again that it's very important that nobody goes far from the house until the dog has the track and has run it a good distance away. Does anybody have any questions?"

Nobody did.

"All right, then. Preacher," he motioned toward Snodgrass, who lifted his hat in acknowledgement. "Maybe you'd lead us in a prayer, sir."

It was just like my daddy. I probably wouldn't have even thought of having prayer, but he did, and he didn't care what anybody thought about it, either. So the preacher stepped up on the porch and poured out his baritone voice, asking the Lord to give us His help. He only spoke for a minute, but I felt better for it.

A man in a group behind me muttered, "We're gonna need all the prayin' we can get, if them two little boys and that coon hound are the best hope we got of findin' that girl."

And in that second I knew we were going to find her, Simmer and Runt and me. The preacher's prayer had put heart in me and stilled part of the butterfly fluttering inside. Then when I heard the scornful remark from behind me, it somehow summed up everything I'd been hearing—and thinking—about myself for most of the years of my life.

I was a runt. My dog was a runt too, a little half-breed misfit, neither coon dog nor man dog. But now the chips were down, and that man was right. They had no better hope than us to find Rosebud. And we would find her. We would find her because we had to. And because we had asked the Lord to help us.

Daddy turned to me. "You ready, Kit?"

167

"Yessir."

"Then start your dog."

"Wait a minute." Deacon Harlow spoke from behind Daddy. He was holding something out to him. "Would this help?" he asked.

Then I saw. It was a little rag doll with bright red yarn hair. I had seen Rosebud play with it a dozen times. She had called it Mandy.

Daddy took the doll and handed it to me. "Kit?"

"It might help, come to think of it, Daddy." The doll would be loaded with Rosebud's scent. I stuffed Mandy into the pocket of my overalls.

Then we started. There was only about an hour of good daylight left, so I was in a sweat to pick up a track and run. The crowd in the yard was quiet as Runt and I made a circle around the house at a distance of about a hundred yards. Runt's nose was on the ground, then in the air, then on the ground again. I could tell he was sorting out the many different scents hanging around the place, looking for one distinct enough to follow. We completed the circle, then I walked him fifty yards farther from the house and started a bigger circle. Then I stopped my dog and pulled Mandy from my pocket.

"This is her, Runt," I shoved the doll in his face. "You know Rosebud. She smells like this. Now we got to find her, Runt. She's in trouble and the sun's going down. We got to find her, dog. *Find him!*" Rosie wasn't a "him," of course, but that was the command Runt was used to hearing, so I hollered it at him when I gave him a slack leash. Now we were clear of the confusion of scents near the house and Runt seemed to know exactly who we were looking for. Eagerly he snuffled along at a fast walk, his long ears dangling in his face. I followed, keeping the strap just taut, not holding him back but not rushing him. Out of the corner of my eye I could see the people up at the house watching us, standing quiet except for those loading the wagons to follow us.

We had rounded the back side of the house and made a hundred yards or so across the face of the gentle upward slope of the pasture when Runt hit the trail. I couldn't see any visual sign in the grass, cropped and trampled as it was by the cattle, but there was no doubt Runt was tracking somebody. I felt a rush of excitement through me. He had something! I let him have his head, running to keep him from wearing himself out pulling me. Then I stopped him and reached for Mandy again. Working my way up the strap hand over hand against his indignant tugging, I caught Runt by the harness and rubbed the doll in his face again. He grabbed it out of my hand, whipped it back and forth a second like killing a rat, then flung it down and surged forward again. I snatched up Mandy just as he nearly yanked my arm off hitting the end of the strap. I was sure we were on the trail of Rosebud.

"He's got a track!" I shouted to the house. A babble of excitement swept across the yard and everybody began to drift to the side of the yard toward me, as if they expected to see the scent Runt was following. Simmer, who had waited until now to keep from scattering any more extra scent around, came running to join us.

"Think it's her?" he asked, pounding up behind me all breathless.

"I'm pretty sure it is," I told him. "It's heading down toward the creek, and it would be just like Rosebud to go fooling around down there where she's not s'posed to."

169

We curved down the hill, crossed the pasture fence and the road, and then were in the brushy creek bottom. Back to my left I saw horsemen and the first wagon start easing down the road toward us, keeping a good distance in case the trail headed back their way and they could foul the scent.

Five minutes later I was sure we were following Rosebud. The track twisted and turned just as a little child would. I made up my mind when we came to a huge hollow maple tree standing like a monarch over a clearing lush with thick grass. Honey bees buzzed in and out of a knothole high up the trunk.

"Look how the grass is trampled all around," I said to Simmer, pointing. "She's circled and circled watching the bees."

"Yep," he said, excitedly. "And Runt's having trouble with all the tangled up scent. He can't decide which way she left out of here."

It was true. Runt was swinging back and forth across the trampled area, getting farther and farther from the tree trunk in a search for the track Rosebud had left on. He found it and plunged toward the creek, a few yards away. My heart jumped to my throat. If she had fallen in...

But no. Runt hit the high creek bank at a fast trot, sure of his track and ready to sail ahead. Just a quick snuffle at the edge then he headed hard right and followed the bank upstream. A few yards, and he swerved away from the creek where Rosebud had been forced to detour around some thick bushes crowding the bank. Then he was back at the edge again, then away again and heading upstream.

"She's looking for a place to cross!" Simmer exclaimed.

I thought he was right. Rosebud had wanted to see the other side of the creek, and she had kept moving upstream through the brush and checking at each break in the bushes looking for a low bank and shallow water. She had found it where a spring branch crossed the bottom land and emptied into a shoal of the creek. We found the scrape of her little shoe where she had slipped in the mud beside the branch. Most likely she had waded the last few steps of the branch and then straight across the creek toward the low, gravelly bank on the far side.

I didn't waste time thinking about other ways she might have gone. The easiest walking was across the creek. And that's the way Runt wanted to go, though I could tell he didn't smell anything at the moment. I gave him slack and plunged into the water right behind him, sure that he would hit the track again where Rosebud had come out of the creek. Splashing across, we came out on the other side dripping from the waist down. We would be uncomfortable if it got chilly after sundown.

Sure enough, Runt's nose hit the ground eagerly as soon as we got dirt under us again, and he was off at a gallop toward the bluffs a quarter mile away at the far side of the creek bottom. Just then we heard a splashing in the creek behind us and Bud came thundering up on his long-legged horse.

"How we doing, men?" he asked, thoughtfully keeping some yards distance.

"I just know it's her, Bud. We saw a track in the mud back by the crick, and Runt goes crazy every time I give him a sniff of the doll." I slowed Runt to a reluctant walk so I could talk. "I think she's heading to the bluffs to climb up and look over the valley."

Bud nodded. "Sounds like her, all right. Always climbing up something or crawling into something." He blew out his cheeks and spoke again, low, as if maybe he was talking to himself. "I sure hope Runt can find her. It could get cold tonight and she's wet...Mary Ann's scared sick." He sounded like Mary Ann wasn't the only one scared sick.

It was getting dark now, at least in the shadow of the bluffs west of the creek. Bud followed along with us a few minutes, then wheeled his horse and cantered back toward the road to find some lanterns for us. When he got back, we were almost in need of them.

Rosebud had followed the foot of the bluffs a good way up the creek bottom before she first tried to climb up. When her trail turned upward, I knew we were in for rough sailing. The track was over six hours old, and while that was fine in the damp grass and brush of the creek bottom, the ridge and the bluffs along it were high and dry with lots of gravel and little dirt to hold scent. Runt stuck tight to the narrow game trail Rosebud had chosen, winding slowly higher along the hill face as we fought our way up toward where the last glinting rays of the setting sun were setting fire to the early fall colors in the leaves. Bud called from below, "Hold up a minute, Kit. Simmer, come on back down and get some light."

I pulled Runt to a stop, grateful for a minute's rest. Simmer retraced his steps along the rocky path to where Bud sat on his horse, lighting the lanterns he had brought.

"I don't know if I can carry a light, Bud," I hollered. "I've got my hands full with the dog."

"Simmer may have to carry both of 'em part of the time," he called back. "But I'm afraid for you not to have a spare if you get too far away for me to get to you."

He was right. Within half an hour we were on the ridge above the bluffs, winding our way through the oaks and cedars that clung to the rocky slope. With daylight we would have had a big view of the creek bottom all the way back to Harlows' and a long way upstream. The sun was long gone now and twilight was turning to darkness. Far away and below we could tell where the road was by the lanterns and torches that flickered and glowed, looking almost like lightning bugs in the distance. Whippoorwills were calling and my feet were getting cold from their soaking in the creek.

Runt was going slower now, not from fatigue as much as the difficulty of finding scent on the rocky path. For another hour we worked our way steadily along, twisting and turning among the trees and boulders. Then the track turned downhill again, angling slowly back toward the bottom of the bluffs.

But now the ground was different. Runt was leading us down a trail that formed a kind of trough between the bottom of the bluffs and a long line of jagged boulders. Soil had washed down into the narrow hollow so that we were once again on real dirt. Runt responded to the thicker scent with a burst of speed that soon had me trotting to keep up. I began to feel hopeful.

"Look, Simmer!" I called over my shoulder. "He's going better than he was down in the bottom—I think we're getting hot!"

And that's sure the way it looked. I knew that our fear for Rosebud had kept us moving a lot faster than any seven-

173

year-old girl could get through those woods. Besides, Runt was plowing along with new energy, snuffling and snorting as he plunged ahead confidently. I was shivering in my wet overalls, but my hopes began to rise. We were getting closer to Rosebud. Now if she just hadn't managed to get herself hurt somehow...

Our speed picked up even more as we hit a steeper downward grade. We galloped along in Runt's wake, the two lanterns casting ghostly moving shadows among the trees and boulders with their yellow light. We hugged the rocky wall of the bluff for a few yards as the passage narrowed even more, then we rounded a sharp turn in the trail and suddenly Runt stopped as if he had hit a brick wall. I was running far too fast to stop; my breath was coming in ragged gasps and my lungs were burning from trying to drag enough air into them. I crashed into Runt and went flying tip over teakettle over his head.

I learned that night how much can happen in about half a second. Scared and shocked as I was to suddenly collide with Runt like that, still I saw enough to know instantly what had happened. And terror exploded in me like dynamite in that tiny piece of time it took me to fly over Runt's head and smash right into the reason he had stopped. A huge raccoon hunkered in the middle of the path.

In the half second before my lantern went smashing among the rocks, I saw both the coon and the reason he hadn't heard us coming. He had been busily trying to gnaw his way into a terrapin—which is what we call box turtles—that had seen him coming in time to get his shell closed. The coon had been grappling around with the turtle, rattling it among the rocks as he scrambled to get a tooth started somewhere. Likely he was just as surprised as we were at our sudden meeting, and just as unhappy, too.

All in the same half second, I saw that this was the biggest coon I had ever seen. Simmer later swore that the thing would have weighed forty pounds if it weighed an ounce. But it wasn't the size that terrified me. It was the fact that I knew Runt would now panic and fall to pieces. We would lose our only hope of finding Rosebud before daylight.

I hit the ground hard, my right shoulder striking the coon and knocking him kitty-wampus. But all in that same half second, he scrambled to his feet and leaped on me with a squall. He was just panicked enough to feel cornered and when that happens to a coon, he's going to light into something fang and claw. I rolled and hollered, striking out with hands and feet in a desperate bid to get in a lick that would knock the coon back and give me a chance to get up. I could hear Simmer yelling behind me but I knew the passage between the rocks was too narrow to let him get close with a rock or club. The coon was biting and clawing at me like a demon, opening deep gashes in my face and scalp as I scrabbled on the ground. Then suddenly he was off me.

It was because of Runt. I heard a strangled roar from my dog then felt one of his big paws punch me hard in the ribs as he tore over and past me. He slammed into the coon and the air was full of squalling and snarling as the two of them shredded each other's hides. I got my feet under me and left them to it, knocking Simmer back a step as I reeled backward in pain and shock. Then, just as suddenly, it was over.

The coon, after having mixed it up with first me and then Runt, seemed to feel that he was outnumbered and the turtle wasn't worth fighting over. He rolled free from Runt for an instant, leaped to the top of a nearby boulder and was gone in the darkness.

Simmer got an arm around me and helped me sit down on a boulder. His eyes were big and he looked pale even in the yellow lantern light.

"Laws a-mercy, Kit, are you all right?" He must have been as scared as I was, if such a thing was possible. "I thought that coon was a-gonna claw your eyes out!"

I couldn't talk for a minute so we sat there leaning on each other and trying to get our breath back. Beyond the reach of the lantern I heard Runt's claws scratching on the rocks as he sent the coon off with a parting growl, then he was back, shoving his nose into my middle, whining and sniffing and licking me as if afraid I might be bleeding to death. I got a shaking arm around him and pounded him lovingly with my other hand.

"Runt! Oh, Runt ol' boy! You sure saved my bacon. Oh, Runt," I went on babbling like that for a few minutes, hugging and petting him, gasping for breath, halfway crying. Then suddenly I stood up, turned and leaned far over the rock I'd been sitting on to heave my share of Mama's chicken and potatoes among the bushes on the downhill slope. I was pretty shaken up.

Simmer grabbed Runt's harness to keep him from wallowing me around until I could pull myself together. We sat a few more minutes and as soon as I could stop shaking I said, "Simmer, we've got to get him started again. We've got to find Rosebud."

"Are you sure you can make it, Kit? You're pretty cut up." He hung his lantern on a dead limb, pulled his bandana out and dabbed at a cut on my forehead with it.

I grimaced as he touched raw flesh. "I've got to make it. I don't know if Runt will start again or not, but if he will I don't think he'll go far away from me after all this."

I stood up and tried my balance. I felt all right except that my insides were still cramping a little and I had burning, stinging cuts on my head and hands. My left earlobe was split but not bleeding much. I bent over to pick up Runt's dragging leash, then had to sit down again as a wave of dizziness washed over me. I took several long, deep breaths then carefully stood up again.

"Find him, Runt!" I commanded, starting down the path toward the creek again. And lo and behold, after just a few steps Runt passed me, his nose in the dirt and sniffing up a storm. He was back after Rosebud!

For a long time after that night it was a subject of discussion among the hound men along Flat Creek, how in the world a soured coon dog could act the way Runt had. What had made him attack the coon after having stopped dead still at sight of it? Was it just the fighting heart of a varmint hound showing itself in the grown dog after having been beaten down in the puppy? Or had Runt's fear for me overcome his fear for himself and driven him into the fight? I'll never really know.

But it's been interesting since then to watch Runt when Daddy nails a fresh coonskin to the shed wall or we're rambling along the creek and find coon tracks in the mud. Since the night of the hunt for Rosebud I've never known him to show the slightest fear of a coon.

But I've never seen him chase one, either.

Chapter 15

TRAPPED IN THE CAVE

By the time we tracked Rosebud back to the creek bottom my wounds had all quit bleeding and I'd gotten used to the pain enough that I felt I could go on a good while yet. Bud rode up to us out of the dark, having followed our lantern's progress up and back down the ridge. He gave a sharp whistle when he saw me.

"Good night, what happened to you, Kit?"

We told him about the coon fight. He looked worried.

"You think Runt'll go on and track after that?" he asked.

"He seems to be all right now," I assured him. "He acts like he's forgot all about it." I hoped that was true. But I sure hadn't.

Again Bud stayed with us, riding along a few yards off to the side, on "coon watch," he said. Off to our right we could see the lanterns again, drifting along the road and roughly keeping up with our progress. We marched wearily on, Runt pulling steadily through the thick grass. I began to notice we were heading back toward the creek.

"I think she's going to ford the crick again," I said to nobody in particular. That direction would take us back toward the road where the rest of the men were sitting in their wagons and on their horses, no doubt impatiently, waiting until the time came when they could do something to help.

Sure enough, the track led across the creek and angled diagonally across the fields toward the road. With Runt forging ahead and sure of himself, I could take my attention away from him and speculate on where Rosebud might be headed. When it came to me, I stopped dead in my tracks and almost fainted. Runt, jerked suddenly to a stop, looked around to see what the trouble was. I stood stock still and forgot to breathe. Rosebud was headed for Ash Cave.

They say there are two hundred caves in the limestone hills of southern Missouri. I don't know about that, but there are several within an easy horseback ride of my house. Ash Cave, located on the road between our home and Cassville, is one of the best known. A lot of soldiers camped there during the war and it's always been a favorite haunt for adventurous farm boys for I guess as long as there have been farm boys around here. The mouth of the cave is separated into a double opening by a huge column of stone, and either of the openings is big enough to drive a team and wagon through. But the main passage grows smaller and smaller the farther back in it you go, until you pop out of a little hole into daylight some distance up the hill above the entrance. It's a twisting, turning, crawling, squeezing tunnel before you're through, and enough to make you nervous if you're not used to tight places. Most of the local boys had been through it at least once, and I was one of a few who had been through without a light.

179

Now it looked as if Miss Rose Marie Harlow had decided to try her skill.

The more I thought about it, the more sure I became that Ash Cave was her destination. It was only a quarter of a mile ahead, and it would have been easily visible from a number of places along her path that afternoon.

"Bud!" I called. "Come here, quick!"

Bud came jogging his horse into the circle of lantern light.

"What's the matter, Kit?"

"Bud, I think Rosebud's gone into the cave. We're heading straight toward it and that's just the kind of place she'd pick to play."

He frowned doubtfully. "I dunno, Kit. Deacon Harlow sent a man in there this afternoon when they first missed her. He hollered around for a while but nobody answered."

"But was that early in the afternoon? Maybe the man went there while she was still in the woods. If she went in the cave after that, nobody would've thought to check again."

Bud chewed on that one a minute. Then he turned his horse toward the lightning bugs on the road.

"Kit, you keep your dog on the track. I'll go tell everybody to stay away from the cave 'til Runt gets there to look it over."

Then he was gone into the dark, cantering across the field as fast as I'd have dared to ride in daylight.

We were close enough now to hear snatches of talk from the men in the road. There was some excitement among them as they grouped around Bud to hear what he had to say. More lightning bugs kept bobbing toward him until we could plainly see him on his horse and the men gathered around listening.

Then we were crossing the road and approaching the yawning entrance to the cave. Runt was pulling steadily toward it, nose to the ground, ears dangling, the loose skin of his forehead wrinkling into the comical frown that at other times looked so funny to me. Tonight I hardly noticed. I was thinking about that cave.

When Runt entered the cave it was plain as the nose on your face that Rosebud had been in it recently and that she had wandered all around in the big chamber by the entrance. Runt had no sooner gotten inside than he began to run back and forth sniffing, whining, wagging his crooked hound tail. His nose was up and down, now in the air and now on the ground. Her scent must be hanging all over.

I didn't let him go far back in the cave. Instead I took him outside and walked him back and forth in front of the entrance to see if he'd pick up a trail leading back out. He didn't. He kept wanting to go back in the cave.

Sometime that afternoon, Rosebud Harlow had gone in there and she hadn't come out.

I yelled her name but either there was no answer or she was too far back for me to hear her. Runt was no help, whining and clawing around in the rocks wanting to find Rosebud and making so much racket echo around the place you couldn't have heard anything much quieter than a gunshot. I dragged him outside and handed his strap to Simmer, who had waited for me at the cave entrance.

"Here, hold him a minute, will you? I'm whipped out."

I hollered for Bud again and he came at a gallop along the road. My father rode beside him on Chip. Daddy had remembered to wear his badge tonight.

"She's in the cave," I told them.

"Son, are you sure?" Daddy asked.

"I"m sure." I nodded. "Runt pulled me straight to the cave and he was all excited sniffing around in there. I brought him out and walked him up and down the creek both ways but he couldn't find a track coming out. She's in there."

They were off their horses in a second and handing their reins to me.

"Wait out here, boys," Daddy said.

They took the lantern from Simmer and hurried through the arch. We heard their boots scraping on the rocks and gravel, then there was a second of silence and my father shouted.

"Rooooosebuuuuuud!" The echoes bounced around inside the cave for an hour, it seemed like, then it got deathly quiet again. Evidently Daddy thought he had heard an answer, because he was quiet for a minute, then tried it again.

"Rosebud!" He must be making it shorter to help with the echo, I thought.

Then we heard it. A short, faint, high-pitched cry from deep within the cave. The echoes must have covered it after Daddy's first yell, but this time there was no doubt. My almost little sister was there and she was alive.

Daddy and Bud reappeared, the lantern swinging wildly as they hurried.

"Bud, go get the men and make sure we've got some candles. There may be places in there too tight for a lantern." Daddy turned to me. "Kit, let's take Runt back in there and see if he can tell us which tunnel she's in."

Bud jerked his reins out of my hand and threw himself aboard his horse without using the stirrup. Then he was gone in a pounding of hooves down the dark road.

Simmer handed me Runt's strap back. "You want me to do anything, Sheriff?" he asked Daddy.

"Just hold my horse, Simmer. And don't let anybody but Bud come inside until we're ready for 'em, Simmer."

I could see that made Sim feel proud, having that kind of responsibility. He stood up real tall and shortened up on Chip's reins. He almost smiled a little.

I took Runt down the main passage first, thinking that was most likely the place Rosie would pick to explore, but he only trotted a few yards down it and quit, turning to shove past me and retrace his steps. Back in the big chamber, he followed the wall on our left, his shadow in the lantern light walking along it until he reached the place where it was split by a huge crevice, like a jagged crack in the inside of the hill.

That was where he wanted to go. He lunged into the crack, dragging the leash tight against the corner of rock before I could make the turn with him. I stopped him then, using the friction of the rock to my advantage, and then stepped around behind him and began dragging him back. He fought me every inch, whining and scrabbling with his paws trying to find traction among the rocks. Finally I got him out and led him around the chamber again, making him take time to check out every nook and cranny among the ragged layers and formations of rock. But all the time he was trying to drag me back to that crack. I stopped him just short of pulling me in there again.

"So that's it." My father's voice sounded grim. His face looked grim too, in the glow of the smoky lantern. He stepped past me into the passage. I pulled Runt farther back to make room.

Daddy hollered again. "Rosebud!"

There was less echo with him hollering in that smaller passage and in a second I heard her answer, "I'm here!" Her voice was tiny and thin and muffled. It made me think of somebody calling from deep in a coal mine.

There was no point trying to talk to her; she couldn't hear us any better than we could hear her.

Daddy turned to me. "Come on, Kit."

Dragging Runt, who still wanted to go back after Rosebud, I followed him out of the cave and here came what looked like the whole population of Barry County. Dozens of torches and lanterns bobbed along toward us, making it bright as day for several yards on either side of the road. It looked like a long torchlight parade, with people walking and riding in wagons and buggies and on horseback. They were close enough that I could recognize faces. Simmer's father was in the lead, driving the wagon with the supplies in it. He had two other neighbors on the wagon with him. Right behind him came the Harlows' fancy carriage pulled by two sleek bays, and in it Deacon and Mrs. Harlow and Miss Mary Ann. Bud rode along beside them, turning in his saddle now and then to keep other people from crowding ahead. I handed Runt's strap to somebody, I forget now who, and asked him to tie him up.

They all stopped in front of the cave and the crowd surged forward with a babble of voices. I noticed there weren't any kids present. Bud must have made them stay

184

down at the Harlow place. Daddy turned on his sheriff volume again.

"Everybody stay where you are!" he thundered. Everybody stopped talking. "The child is in this cave, and I want only her family and the men I call by name inside. Everybody else stay out. We'll be sending somebody out to let you know what's going on every few minutes."

The crowd stood still then and the babble was quieter when it started up again. A bonfire was started and people gathered around it to fight the chill of the night.

Daddy called for some lights and led Deacon Harlow and the women inside the cave, explaining in quiet tones what he knew so far and what he was planning to do.

"I'm going to send Bud in there to bring her out," he was saying. "She's far enough back that we can't talk to her, so I don't know whether she's hurt in any way. But I'm told the doctor is now on his way from town, so we'll see that she gets whatever she needs. Now my suggestion is that you two ladies wait out by the fire where you'll be a little more comfortable. Charles," he said to Deacon Harlow, "if you want to stay and help, that's fine. If you'd rather stay with your wife and daughter, go ahead. We've got plenty of men."

Mrs. Harlow looked around at the gloomy inside of the cave.

"I believe I will wait outside, Charles," she told her husband. "If there's nothing I can do in here."

"I'll wait with her." The voice came from behind us. There was my mama, walking in through the rocky arch of the cave's entrance. She was wearing her bonnet and cape, and I got the feeling she had been staying close to Mrs. Harlow for quite a while that evening.

Mama led her out, but Miss Mary Ann touched her father's sleeve and said, "I'd rather wait in here with you if that's all right, Papa."

The Deacon looked at Daddy. "That's fine, Charles, if that's what the two of you want," Daddy told him.

Then Bud came in carrying a burlap sack with a bunch of candles in it.

"Ready, Bud?" my father asked him.

"Yep." Bud sat down on a point of rock and unbuckled his spurs. Then he took off his gun belt. He handed them to me. "Would you put these in my saddle bag, Kit?"

Then he lit a candle off the lantern my father was holding, gave Mary Ann an encouraging smile, and started back into the crevice. He could only walk a few feet before the passage shrank to crawling height and he dropped to his hands and knees.

I ran out and put Bud's things in his saddle bags, then took Daddy's horse from Simmer and tied him to a tree.

I took Simmer back into the cave with me. Daddy and the Harlows were standing silently, listening to the scuffing and grunting sounds coming from the tunnel. Then Bud hollered to Rosebud. His voice sounded strange and muffled, as voices will in such places. If Rosie answered him, we couldn't hear her. Another couple of minutes went by. We heard more scuffling, then Bud called again, more muffled this time.

There was silence for a minute, then the scraping and scuffling started again. Finally, Bud's head appeared. His face looked bleak. His candle was out, there were scrape marks on his forehead and he was smeared with clay and dust. Deacon Harlow offered a hand and helped him to his feet.

186

"I can't get to her," he said, breathing heavily. "There's at least one place where the tunnel is too narrow. She probably got through pretty easy, but it's 'way too tight for me." He stood beside Miss Mary Ann and looked at her apologetically, as if he felt that it was his fault.

"Could you talk to her?" Deacon Harlow asked.

"Yes sir, I could. I told her not to worry, that we were here to get her out and everything would be all right. I asked if she was hurt or anything and she said she hurt her ankle. Said she's down in a hole and can't climb out. Says she's cold."

Daddy asked him, "Any idea how far back she is?"

"I'd say I was about halfway to her. And I was maybe thirty or forty feet back, I think."

"Does it slope down?"

"A little. Not a whole lot."

"Floor of the tunnel rough?"

"Yeah. Pretty rough."

Daddy thought a minute. "Well, we're just going to have to send somebody smaller in there. That leaves me out, and you, too, Charles."

He looked around as if he was about to walk outside and ask for a volunteer. Then his eye fell on me, standing there beside Simmer. And then I noticed they were all looking at me.

"Think you could do it, Kit?" Daddy asked.

I didn't know what to say. I had run and walked through the brush for miles that evening, lost some blood in a fight with an angry coon, gotten throroughly chilled after wading the creek and heaved my supper all over a rocky hillside. I was feeling a little puny and I quite honestly didn't know just what I could do.

187

So I said, "I'll try." It was all I knew to say.

Miss Mary Ann looked at me, her eyes shining as she hung on Bud's arm. "Oh, thank you, Kit," she said, and for some reason I felt my face get all red and go to burning. I was ready to go crawl in a hole then.

Daddy called for a rope and tied it to one of my ankles. Bud gave me six candles and a box of matches. I lit one of the candles, then stuck the others, along with the matches in my back pockets.

"I'd suggest you light a candle and leave it burning every few yards if you can," Bud told me. I stepped into the passage and got down on all fours. I started crawling.

I had been in this tunnel before; I had been in every crack and crevice in every cave I could get to. I knew the narrow place that had stopped Bud. But I had thought the passage ended just beyond that point. I had poked my head through there once and looked around as much as I could, but the top and bottom rock seemed to squeeze tighter and tighter together a few feet beyond, so that there didn't seem to be any tunnel left. There must be a side passage.

Caves aren't like you might think they are if you've only read about them in books. I read a book once about some boys lost in a cave, and the pictures in the book showed nice, neat tunnels with level floors and rounded ceilings. Caves aren't really like that, at least not the caves in Barry County. Cave passages might be round part of the way and deep v-shaped slashes in the rock somewhere else. Sometimes they get real small just before opening into huge chambers. Sometimes they're just cracks between stone walls. Sometimes you're crawling on smooth stone, sometimes mud or gravel or fist-size rocks. You never know what the inside of a cave will be like, but it won't often be neat and level.

The passage I was in was the usual jumble of rock. I crawled along as fast as I could, the candle dripping hot tallow on my hand sometimes, banging my head and elbows and knees painfully. Part of the time I traveled on hands and knees, part of the time worming on my belly, now and then able to stand in a hunched-over position to get around or over some rocky outcropping. It didn't take long to get to the place that had stopped Bud. The ceiling was about three feet high there; there was room to get through that way if I could maybe turn sideways to make my shoulders pass. I backed off a few feet and set up a candle by dripping some tallow on a point of the rock wall and sticking the candle butt in the tallow. Lighting it with the stub of candle I had been using, I started back for the tight place and stuck the stub through.

"Rosebud!" I yelled.

Her little thin voice came back to me. It was the prettiest sound I'd ever heard.

"Is that Kit?" Muffled, but clear.

"Yes, it's me, Rosie! I'm coming to get you!" I took a minute to get my breath. Rosie sounded all right. She must be all right. I rolled over on my back and grinned at the solid rock above me. Rosie was all right. I felt like laughing and crying and shouting and jumping up and down. Little Rosebud was all right. I just had to get her out of here.

I heard her yelling again, sounding far away. "I'm in a hole, Kit!"

I yelled back, so she'd know I heard her and was still here. "I'll get you out, Rosie! Just a minute!"

189

Now I rolled onto my side and hoisted myself up a few inches to where the opening was an inch or two wider. It was awkward. I got a muscle cramp in my left side and dropped my candle, leaving me only light from the candle behind me, which wasn't much. But I made it through, gasping and grunting and losing the button off one of my overall straps. I lit another candle and looked around me.

The passage was a little larger here. I could sit up and look around, but at first I couldn't see how a body could go any farther. Then I spotted it. A crevice in the left wall angling back somewhat in the direction I had come from. You couldn't see it except from this side.

It took some worming, but I made the turn and then was able to travel on my knees. Gravel and slab rock were giving my knees and shins a beating, but I didn't slow down. I called again to Rosie and she answered me. I could hear her clearly now. But still she was beyond the light of my candle.

I set up another candle, propping it up between rocks and lit it. Then I started crawling again. Twenty feet farther on I found Rosie.

The bottom dropped out of the passage and if I hadn't had a light I would have landed right on top of her. The hole she was in was about as big around as a barrel and seven or eight feet deep. The rock sides were steep and didn't offer a lot to hang onto. I stuck my head over the rim and looked down. Rosie sat on the gravel at the bottom of the hole, looking up at me.

Then she smiled. "Hey, Kit," she said.

I lost control then. I was sprawled on my belly on cold rock, weak and sick and tired. I was chewed up and bruised up and bleeding where a bump against cave rock had reopened a cut on my forehead. My nerves were quivering all through me and the rest of me was shaking like a leaf in a strong wind. I left my candle hand hanging over the hole to give Rosie some light, then buried my face in my other arm and cried. I don't know if I'd ever cried harder in my life; I didn't worry about being thirteen and too big for such childishness, I just let go and cried because crying seemed the thing to do.

I heard the gravel crunch as Rosie got to her feet. I wanted to say something to her to reassure her, but all I could do was sob. Finally I got my breath and settled down. I stuck my head over again.

"You about ready to go home, Rosebud?" I asked her. I could see the tracks of tears on her dirty cheeks. I wouldn't let myself think how she must have felt, trapped all that time down there in the dark.

"I want Mommy," she said, and fresh tears started on her upturned face.

"Well, let's go see her right now." I had to start headfirst, but by bracing my hands against the far wall of the hole I was able to turn around and back down. I noticed that the passage continued beyond the hole, but I didn't even look to see where it went. Carefully shielding my candle, I dropped to the gravel beside Rosebud.

Rosie flung her arms around me and cried louder. "I was scared, Kit! And I'm so cold!"

I hugged her tightly and patted her back, pulling her little face into my chest.

"It's all right Rosie. It's all right, it's all right." I didn't know what I was supposed to say, so I just kept telling her it was all right, over and over.

191

Then I lit a fresh candle. I only had a couple more, I noticed. I looked her all over for hurts, but all I saw was stone bruises and briar scratches and her left ankle, which was swollen and purple. Her crying slowly subsided and she smiled at me through her sniffles.

"I'm glad you came for me, Kit. I like it when you come to see me."

"I like coming to see you, too, Rosebud. Now, you think you can crawl out of here?"

"If you'll help me out of this hole I can."

"Good. Let me rest a minute and I'll heft you out." Then I thought to ask her, "Rosebud, how on earth did you get down here, anyway?"

"I was esploring."

"You were exploring in the dark?"

"No, silly, I had a candle. But it's all burned up."

"Where'd you get a candle?"

"I brought it from home."

"You brought—you mean you were headed for this cave when you left home?"

"Uh-huh. I like esploring caves."

"But—then why in creation did you cross the creek and tramp all over the ridge on the other side?"

"I was esploring over there, too."

"Well, let's 'esplore' our way back home. Here, let me help you up. Grab on up top when you can reach it.

I stuck my candle in a crack in the rock and hoisted her up, being ever so careful of her ankle. She gingerly crawled out the top of the hole, then turned around on her hands and knees and looked down at me.

"Kit?"

"What, knucklehead?"

"Will you be my beau?"

That was too much. I leaned my forehead against the rock wall and sobbed again, bringing the heaves up from way down in my shoes. I tried to keep it silent so as not to scare her. When I finally could talk again, I didn't look up. I hoped my voice was almost normal when I answered her.

"Yes, Rosebud. I'll be your beau."

Right then I'd have been her elephant if she'd wanted me to.

"Goody!" she cried, and turned to crawl toward the candle I'd left burning back in the passage way. Scraping for a toehold in the rock, I heaved myself up and followed her.

Chapter 16

GOD KNEW BETTER

K-k-chik. Snap. K-k-chik. Snap. K-k-chik. Snap.

I strained to think what the sound was that I kept hearing over and over.

K-k-chik. Snap. K-k-chik. Snap.

It seemed that I should know it, it was familiar. A metallic, sharp sound of parts interacting with each other. Bolts sliding, springs tripping, levers moving, little steel mechanisms being worked in place together, like maybe a lock locking. Then a hard metal snap. K-k-chik. Snap.

It was right beside me; all I'd have to do was open my eyes and the mystery would be solved. But there was a bright light outside my eyelids and they wouldn't open to let it in. I'd wait just a minute and then give a try at making my eyes work.

Now there were voices.

"He's waking up." Mama.

Try the eyelids. Not too quick, just flutter them open in little bits.

K-k-chik. Snap.

Then I was able to see, at least a little. When the glare faded and the fog cleared in front of my face, I saw Simmer. He was grinning at me from a chair beside the bed. My bed. In my room at home. The afternoon sun was streaming in my west window, making it hard to open my eyes.

But I could see Simmer grinning and holding something in his hands that made the sound. K-k-chik. Snap.

Then it all came into focus. Simmer was holding a Winchester rifle in his hands, working the lever action to cock it. K-k-chik. Then he'd pull the trigger and the hammer would fall on the firing pin. Snap. No bullets in it, just cocking the gun and pulling the trigger. Dry firing.

"Well, do you like it?" He was still grinning.

I blinked and opened my eyes wider. Then I saw that the room was full of people. Mama, Daddy, Deacon Harlow, Bud and Miss Mary Ann all sat or stood around me, smiling smiles that looked maybe relieved, as if they'd just found out something they feared might happen wasn't going to. They were smiling at me.

All except Simmer Downs, who was wearing a full-grown grin, still working the lever action of that Winchester. K-k-chik. Snap.

"Simmer," I tried to talk to him. My lips felt thick and sleepy. "Is—is that your gun?"

"Nope," he said. "It's yours. Mine's leaning against the wall over yonder."

I half sat up and twisted my head. In the wall corner nearest the door stood another rifle, just like the one Simmer was holding. Two Winchester rifles, just alike. Both looking shiny new. Simmer snapped the hammer of the one he had said was mine once more, then laid it on the bed beside me. I reached out and felt the cool metal of its breech and barrel, the smooth walnut stock. Deacon Harlow spoke up.

"They're part of a gift, Kit. I asked Bud what I could give you and Simmer to show my appreciation for your finding Rose Marie."

Rosebud! Now I remembered. The long, chilling, exhausting night. The track. The coon fight. The cave.

"Is Rosebud all right?" I asked anxiously. I sat fully up against the head of the bed and looked around at everybody.

"She's fine, Kit, thanks to you." It was the closest I had ever seen Deacon Harlow to having tears in his eyes.

Then they told me what I didn't remember. How Rosebud had come crawling out of the crevice carefully dragging her swollen ankle. How I had followed her out, both of us covered with dirt, her hair all tangles and my forehead bruised and bleeding. How Mama and Daddy and Bud and the Harlows had crowded around Rosebud while the mob outside in the bonfire light had cheered. How I had stumbled to my feet and staggered toward Simmer with a crazy grin on my clawed face, raising my right arm as if to start our Official Indian War Dance, and finally how I had collapsed flat on my face in the rocky rubble of the cavern floor before he could catch me.

The doctor had examined Rosebud and me on the hay in one of the wagons, we had been taken home and cleaned up and put to bed. Rosebud had been up in time for breakfast this morning. I was just now coming to, my body a mass of aches and stiffness, in the middle of the afternoon. The main hopeful sign was that I was feeling hungry.

Deacon Harlow said, "If you're up to it, Kit, I'd like you and your parents and Simmer to come up to our place for supper this evening. Bud will be joining us, and by the way, I'd like you to bring Runt. I'll have a steak for him." Everybody chuckled, then he went on. "And one other thing. Come prepared to do some riding. I want you and Simmer to each pick out any horse on the place to keep for your own. That's the other part of the gift."

I looked at Mama and Daddy. They'd say that this was too much; that they couldn't let anybody give their son something as valuable as a horse when he'd already bought him and his best friend brand new rifles. And they would be right, of course; it was worth all we'd gone through and more just to hear that Rosebud was all right.

But Daddy spoke up. "I told him I'd go along with it, Kit. He really wants to do something for you boys, and I don't reckon it'll ruin you." He looked at Simmer. "And I'll make it all right with your folks too, Simmer."

I tried to say the right things to Deacon Harlow, but it came out sounding like babble. The grownups just smiled and joshed Simmer and me about how we'd probably break our necks riding like fools, if we didn't shoot ourselves first. My head was still spinning when they said they'd step out and let me get dressed.

As Mama started to close the door behind her, I swung my legs over and sat up on the edge of the bed. I had to run out right quick and tell Runt all about this, what he had done for the Harlows and for Simmer and me by finding Rosebud. Then Mama stopped and came back in. She sat down on the bed beside me.

"Kit," she asked me, "do you remember the day Runt fought that coon and got soured on coon hunting?"

197

"Yes, Mama, I remember that."

"Do you remember what I told you that day, when I read to you from the Bible how God makes everybody special and that He has good reasons for how he makes us?"

I thought a minute. "Well, you told me that God didn't make a mistake by making me little. You said that I might get big someday but that whether I did or not, God had a plan for me and that it was best."

"And you asked me if I thought God cared about Runt."

"Uh-huh."

"And I said that God cares even about the sparrows, so surely He cares about Runt."

"Uh-huh." I remembered.

"Well, Kit, I want you to think about all that in light of what happened with Rose Marie."

"What do you mean?"

"Well, for one thing, if Runt hadn't been small, someone would have bought him like they did the other pups, and he wouldn't have been here to find Rosie. And if he hadn't been ruined for coons, you never would have trained him to hunt people."

I stared at her. I hadn't thought about any of that. There hadn't really been time yet. Then something else came to me, something that would change the way I felt about myself forever.

I said, "And if I hadn't been little, if I'd been big like Daddy or Bud, I couldn't have gotten in to where Rosebud was."

"That's right, son. You couldn't have gotten her out."

She didn't say any more, just quietly got up and walked out, closing the door behind her. I had the feeling she wanted me to think all those things through on my own. I sat a while longer more on the side of the bed, doing just that. Then I jumped up `as quickly as my sore body would let me and grabbed a clean pair of overalls off the foot of the bed.

I hoped Simmer and Runt were around somewhere close. The three of us had a lot to talk about.

Also by Rick & Marilyn Boyer:

The Hands-on Dad
Rick shares seven Biblical functions for the father and shows how they apply in home education. These important and practical insights can set both Mom and Dad free to be their best for their children.

Home Educating with Confidence
Rick and Marilyn Boyer share their experiences to encourage and equip others. You don't have to be a child psychologist or have a fancy degree to raise godly children.

Fun Projects for Hands-on Character Building
The Boyers share their philosophy of spiritual training with scores of practical, effective, and enjoyable projects.

Yes, They're all Ours
The story of the Boyer family – what life is like with 14 children, and why we chose to live this way. Also includes humorous anecdotes.

Homemade with Love
Marilyn Boyer shares her tried and true recipes for feeding 14 hungry children economically and simply.

The Runt
Rick Boyer shares with young readers the fictional adventures of a boy and his unpromising, mongrel pup. With that scrap of a dog, God teaches what it really means to be a winner.

Bible Curriculum
Character Qualities flashcards
Cards feature a question and picture to color on the front, and a verse on the back. For example: "Why should we choose godly friends?" Answer: "He who walks with wise men shall be wise. But the companion of fools suffers harm." Proverbs 13:20

If/When flashcards
Teach your children what to do in certain situations. For example: "When tempted to hate correction" (Proverbs 12:1)? Answer: "Whoever loves discipline loves knowledge, but he who hates reproof is stupid."

Proverbs flashcards
Teach your children Bible verses from the Book of Wisdom. Each card features a picture for your child to color.

Proverbs for Preschoolers
Children learn the principles in Proverbs while practicing stylus skills, memorizing the alphabet, and coloring.

Proverbs People I & II
Workbooks that use short-answer questions, stories, quizzes, and coloring pages to teach character qualities to children 8 to 12. **Vol I: Vol II:**

Living the Fruitful Life
A Bible study course on how to apply
the fruit of the Spirit to our lives.
For middle-school students.

Power in Proverbs
A self-led concordance study guide for teenagers.

To request a free catalog of the previous books as well as a whole range of Christian home school materials, please contact The Learning Parent at:
(434) 845-8345
2430 Sunnymeade Road
Rustburg, VA 24588
www.TheLearningParent.com